The Coffee Tasting *Guide*

I
COFFEE

The Coffee Tasting *Guide*

An Introduction To:
Sensory Skills

Written &
Illustrated By

Barry Taft

This book is dedicated to Kata, Winter, and Ragnar

ISBN 978-0-578-34135-4 (Print Edition)

ISBN 978-0-578-34136-1 (eBook Edition)

Cover photo by Barry Taft and Natalie Guemez

Illustrations and book design by Barry Taft

Contents

Introduction 8

Part I: Understanding Taste and Flavor

1. The Anatomy of Flavor 16
2. The Science of Taste 23
3. The Sensory Experience 49

Part II: How to Taste Coffee

4. Cupping 78
5. Adding Form to the Process 95
6. Challenging Your Sensory Skills 105

Conclusion 122

Acknowledgements 124

Further Reading 125

References 126

Introduction

On December 31, 1999, I went a New Year's Eve party at my grandparents' barn in central California. They had rented a "café-in-a-vending-machine" to help keep folks awake. I was only ten years old, so I selected "mocha" thinking that meant "hot chocolate." Much to my dismay, this was not the case.

Mixed in with the delicious chocolate was something horrible. It smelled good, but the taste was something I couldn't understand. Why would anyone drink this ashy, bitter poison? Why would anyone do this to chocolate?

Let's just say that coffee did not leave a good first impression on me, but as the effects of caffeine began to set in, I came to an understanding. This is a drug that helps you stay awake, and the foul taste is something you just have to live with if you want to enjoy those effects. I was in my twenties before I reconsidered this opinion.

Despite working in coffee shops when I got out of high school, it took me a few years before I discovered there was a side of the coffee business that was focused on making the coffee itself taste good and not simply masking its inherent disgusting flavor with syrups. Though I drank a lot of coffee at this point in my life, my beverage of choice was the ever practical iced espresso, which I consumed purely as a caffeine delivery method.

As I eventually began to focus less on reckless partying and more on my career and personal development, I had a job interview at a café serving coffee from the Pacific Northwest. It was a wakeup call for me. The manager was shocked at my ignorance of concepts like weighing espresso shots and pour-over coffee. It seemed that the latte-art skills I had been so proud of from my previous jobs were not as impressive as I thought they were. Instead of getting the barista position I wanted, I was offered a position as a cashier. I went back to the job search.

Before my next interview, I made sure to do enough research that I could "talk the talk," which turned out to be a good strategy. I soon started a barista gig at an extremely high volume café with a strong focus on quality. It was lucky that I had been humbled during the job search, because I started this new job with an open mind, eager to learn. During the training I experienced coffee like I'd never had before. Actually tasting flavors in coffee besides "bitter" was eye opening for me to say the least. I found it especially impressive that the coffee we served had tasting notes. This wasn't the same light, medium, or dark stuff I had interacted with before. It was an entirely different animal.

Working in the company of more experienced baristas, I felt out of my depth. This was a drink with a very complex flavor that I had a lot of trouble putting words to, but I got the impression that I was supposed to be able to articulate what I was tasting. Writing tasting notes, at this point, was immensely intimidating.

When I came in for my shift in the afternoon, my morning counterpart would have the tasting notes written out for their espresso dials. Part of the job was re-dialing the espresso for the rest of the day[DC5], and with that I was supposed to come up with my own tasting notes, but I never received any training on this aspect. I don't think anyone did. For me, it was definitely a case of "fake it till you make it," and I initially fell back on the strong bullshitting skills that I had built up in art school.

After that I started taking my time and trying to taste what I was drinking, and I did my best to improve, taking every new nugget of information that I stumbled upon and implementing it. An internet search on how to taste espresso taught me I needed to follow a sip with an inhale through the mouth and an exhale out the nose. At a coffee tasting with New England coffee guru George Howell, I clung to every pearl of wisdom I heard: Hold filter-coffee in your mouth longer after tasting espresso if you want to taste it at all. Use milk as a palate cleanser. I had an array of tips and tidbits I would think about when tasting coffee, but I still didn't really understand how it all worked.

This slow accumulation of tasting knowledge continued throughout my career. Over the decade after my first "real" coffee job, I built a pretty robust cache of knowledge, having made my way through several world-class training and education programs (from the bottom every time, which is how things go in the coffee industry) and actively going out of my way to taste new coffees and expand my palate. I went all in, dedicating my free time outside of work to learning more about coffee and improving my skills.

There is an unreasonable expectation for professionals in the coffee industry to have obtained a set of tasting skills (a "refined palate") through some means other than objective training. Because of this, there can often be machismo and showboating in a quick and assertive declaration of flavors present in the cup. In my experience, this is antithetical to learning and growth.

Additionally, the consumer for whom the coffee industry produces is often thrown right into the deep-end of these tasting athletics without any primer. This can be off-putting, to state it mildly. Bizarre and unrelatable tasting notes are a big reason why pretentious baristas are the butt of so many jokes! What's worse is when someone pays a lot of money for a coffee, they expect to taste what's described. If someone shells out $15 for a coffee and can't taste what they were promised, they call shenanigans. It's as simple as that.

Despite my experience, I always felt as if tasting was my shortcoming. To be honest, I still do. It's never been easy to separate the subjectivity of what makes "good" flavor from the analytical skill of determining what specific flavors are present in the cup. Is the flavor I don't like a defect? Or is it simply a flavor I don't care for, like licorice? How do I know that what I taste as apple is the same as what someone else tastes as apple?

Excellence in tasting is one of the, if not *the most* difficult aspect of coffee, both to learn and to communicate, but the kicker is that tasting is also an integral part of perfecting every other aspect of coffee.

You need to be able to taste in order to dial in a brewing recipe. You need to be able to taste in order to properly refine your roast curves. You need to be able to taste in order to implement any meaningful quality control practices. You need to be able to taste in order to perfect your green coffee growing practices and processing. Even disregarding professional concerns, consumers need to be able to taste in order to be certain that they're not getting ripped off. Everything revolves around tasting, and I think good taste is really the whole point of specialty coffee.

I believe that overcomplication in the area of tasting is a symptom of inexperience and with mastery comes simplicity and elegance. With this book, I'm hoping to break through some of the inherent subjectivity that comes with tasting coffee to get at the core of what it takes to improve.

An important factor for me is that sensory training requires minimal monetary investment. I think it's critical to emphasize that the skill of tasting is not an insider's club; it is accessible to anyone with the desire to learn and the patience to practice, not simply those who are able to shell out hundreds or thousands of dollars for professional tasting and aroma kits or those fortunate enough to have access to an advanced sensory training program. There's a few small investments to make, but none of them has to be a big hit—and some of them you get to eat.

While this book is focused on coffee tasting, a lot of the information can be applied to the wider culinary arts and should be interesting to the general foodie as well as the specialist. The "sensory siblings" section especially will be valuable for anyone interested in expanding and refining their palate, which is a rewarding journey that brings a newfound appreciation to every tasting experience. I should also mention that while this isn't meant to be a training guide for tasting competition, I think the "challenges" section would be a good place to start for those interested in that aspect.

We'll begin with an overview of how taste and flavor work, and how it applies to coffee. We'll take a look at why certain flavors exist in coffee. We'll talk about language, and how it influences our tasting experience. We'll look at coffee's sensory siblings, or items that contain similar flavor compounds. We'll look at cup tasting and the art of tasting coffee. Finally, we'll finish with challenges that will hone your coffee tasting skills.

Tasting coffee is an incredibly complex endeavor, and one cannot improve beyond a certain point without understanding how it all really works. Especially after writing this book (something I always wished existed during my struggles to improve at tasting), I know this to be true.

Tasting needs to be approached with humility and open-mindedness. Human biology says that even the most expert taster cannot be perfect. Every individual has unique flavor perceptions. We're not all going to taste everything there is to taste, and more importantly, we all taste things differently.

I hope you are able to find as much value in this book as I have in putting it together. Let's get into it.

Part I: Understanding Taste and Flavor

1. The Anatomy of Flavor

TASTE

It's important to understand how the sensation of taste is processed by our brain before we can start to pick apart what it is that makes coffee taste the way it does. So, what's going on when we take a sip?

Taste, smell, and somatosensory data combine in our brain to create our flavor perception. But it's our sense of smell, and our related sensory memory, that help us tie the flavors we're tasting now to flavors we've tasted before. That's really what makes up the discipline of tasting things with complex flavor profiles like coffee, tea, wine, or whiskey.

Taste starts when a flavor compound meets with a sensory receptor taste cell. Flavor compounds bind to these sensory cells and are in turn converted into data that is sent via cranial nerves through the brain stem and on to the cortex.[1] There are different types of taste cells to go with the different basic tastes we can perceive. Taste cells are found in groups of fifty or so inside our taste buds.

You can't see taste buds with the naked eye; those bumpy things on your tongue are called papillae. Some papillae are covered in hundreds to thousands of taste buds and surrounded by glands which flush in flavor compounds. We have four types of papillae. Fungiform, foliate, and circumvallate papillae are the ones with taste buds. Filiform papillae don't contain taste buds at all, and simply help us to break food apart. Papillae are distributed at different parts of the tongue, soft palate, pharynx and upper esophagus.[2]

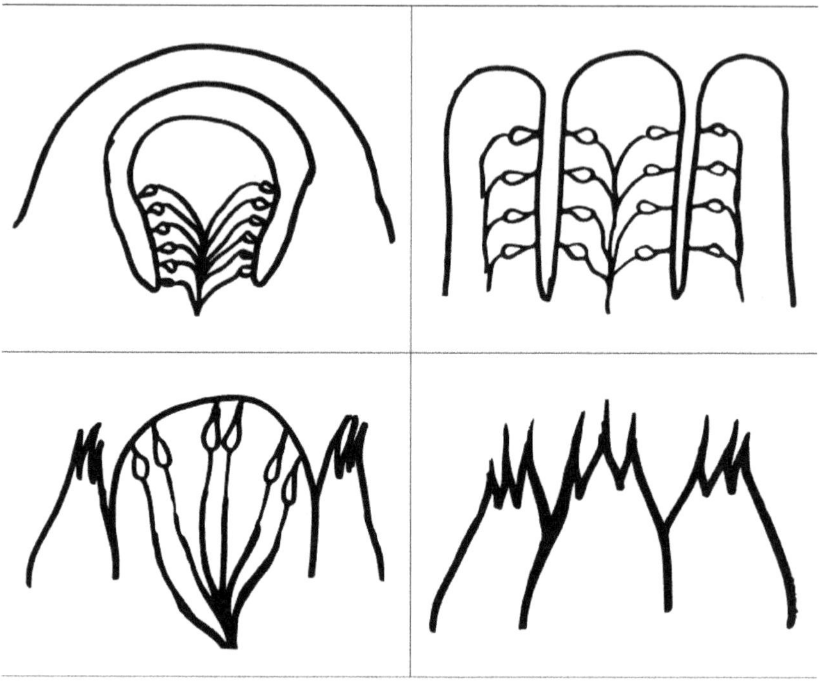

The taste pathway to the brain goes like this:

Taste cells – Taste compounds pass through pores in the specialized mucosa layer of the epithelium covering the papillae and taste buds. They travel down tiny hairs called microvilli, where the compounds bind with taste cells within the taste bud.

Cranial nerve relay – Taste information is relayed via cranial nerves through the thalamus, which is like a sensory information relay hub to the rest of the brain.

Primary gustatory (taste) cortex – This is the part of the brain where we have end receptors for the five basic flavors (sweet, sour, bitter, salt, and umami, as well as receptors for viscosity, texture, temperature, and capsaicin) and where we trans late the signals we've received from our taste cells into something we understand. The primary gustatory cortex is located in the front part of the insula (a central interior part of the brain).

Orbitofrontal cortex – Located in the prefrontal cortex right above the eyes, this is where we combine taste information with other signals from the brain, like smell, audio-visual information, and emotion. The orbitofrontal cortex is the part of the brain that assesses perceived pleasantness and computes reward value to help guide our feeding behavior. It is the same in other mammals, too.[3]

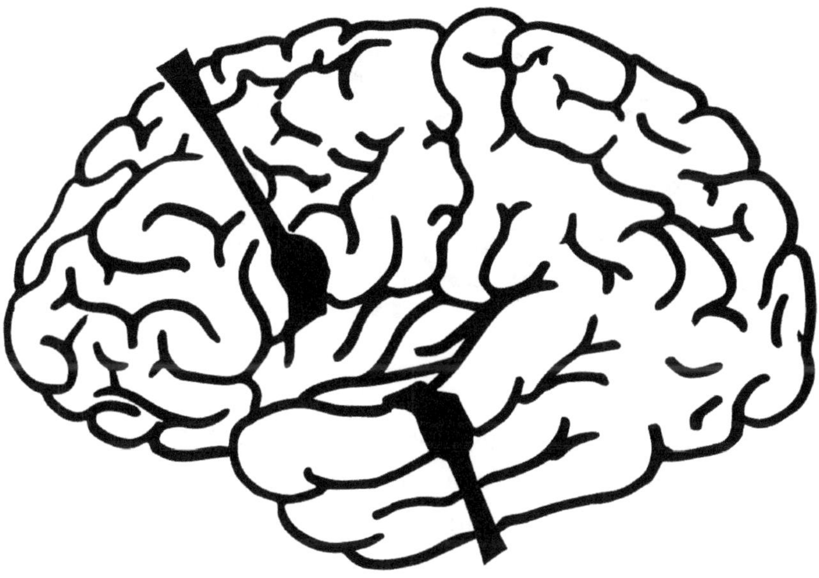

SMELL

There are two different ways that we bring odors into our olfactory (smelling) system. Orthonasal olfaction is "smelling" as we think of it. As we breathe in, aromatic compounds enter the olfactory system directly through the nostrils. Retronasal olfaction is "mouth smell." When food or liquids are in our mouth, aromatic compounds enter the olfactory system through the back of the mouth, and are conveyed to the brain along with taste and somatosensory information (temperature, texture, sound).

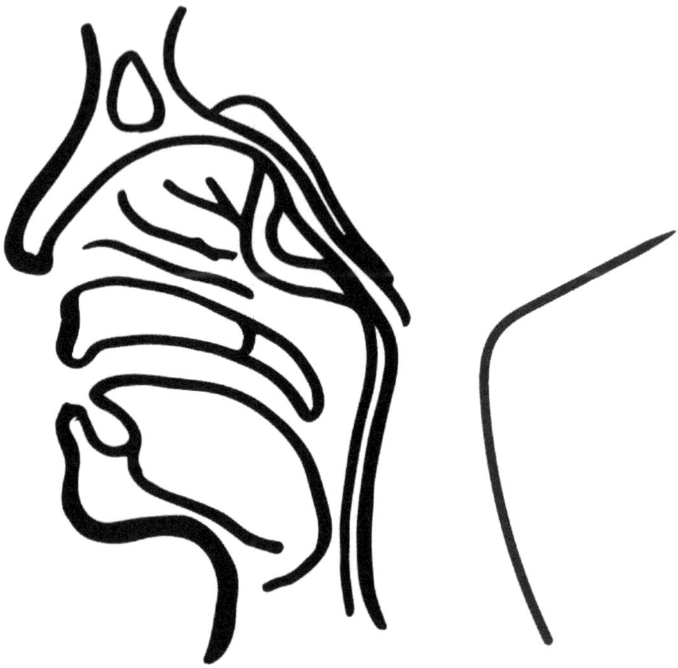

Either way, aromatic compounds enter the olfactory system, they then follow a specific pathway in our brain that is unique from our other neural sensory pathways:

Olfactory receptors – These are located in the olfactory epithelium (a small part of the surface on the top of our nasal cavity) where we begin collection of smell data.

Olfactory bulb – The olfactory bulb takes input from sensory receptors to compile odor information. This information is sent along the olfactory tract to the primary olfactory cortex.

Primary olfactory cortex (rhinencephalon) – The primary olfactory cortex is composed of connections to the amygdala (the epicenter of our emotions), the prefrontal cortex, and the piriform cortex. The piriform cortex is the place where our brain turns the smell data into information we can understand. Unlike our other senses (taste, touch, hearing, and sight), smells bypass the thalamus (sensory hub). This direct connection to the amygdala without going through the thalamus is thought to be the reason we have visceral sensory memories related to smell.[4]

We have an extremely strong connection between smell and memory, which is why specific smells can take us right back to a moment long ago. The unique sensory pathway that smells take in our brains might also be part of the reason we have such a hard time putting names to particular smells, because the sensory data takes a roundabout path before reaching our language center.

Having trouble putting a name to smells doesn't mean humans are particularly bad at smelling. In fact, we have a very acute sense of smell, even compared to animals that are thought to have very refined senses of smells, like dogs. While it doesn't help that our noses can be elevated some five feet off the ground and face downwards, while a dog's nose is right down at the ground where the interesting smells are, the main difference is that humans have let their sense of smell take a back burner to the sexier senses like sight and hearing.

We use our strong sensory memory, fueled by our olfactory system, to play a mental matching game. Therefore, it's absolutely critical to remember to breathe when we're tasting, and to breathe thoughtfully, taking a breath in through the mouth, then out the nose after swallowing to better facilitate retronasal olfaction. The olfactory connection is also why we're terrible at tasting when we've got sinus congestion, or if there is an overwhelming smell in the room.

The fact that there is a distinct difference between the sense of tasting and the discipline of tasting flavors (combining taste and aroma) is a problem with the English language. It can be a little bit tricky to disconnect. Just remember that the sense of taste itself is not the most important piece to get down. So what's the most important factor in the discipline of tasting? As the great actor/sage Tairy Greene wisely said, "It's your nose! Write that down."

2. The Science of Taste

The coffee beverage as we know it is relatively young, coming into being in the 15th century in Yemen, and only exploding in popularity in Europe during the 17th century. By contrast, wine had already been well established by the time the pyramids were built in Ancient Egypt during the 3rd millennium BC. This is part of the reason coffee tasting at any high level is not well established, as best practices, systems, and standards have not had time to develop to the level of a truly ancient culinary art like wine.

Another reason is because coffee is an extremely aromatically complex beverage. Brewed coffee contains more than 1,000 aromatic and flavor compounds, five times that of wine. This is why describing the complex flavors of different coffees is very challenging. It's so challenging, in fact, that flavor description is a key scoring component in barista and brewer competitions.

So what exactly is it that we're tasting, here? The flavor of coffee (or anything else we put in our mouths) is broken up between the basic tastes we take in through our taste cells and volatile (evaporated at room temperature) aromatic compounds we take in through our olfactory system. The basic tastes are very simple to identify. The complication with tasting comes with the staggering number of aromatic compounds, producing untold combinations that muddle together and confuse our senses. That's why any measured approach to tasting must start with the basic tastes, gradually building on them to come up with a more complex picture of the flavor (taste + aroma).

THE BASIC TASTES

The basic tastes are sweet, sour, bitter, salty, and umami. They are triggered by a specific chemical compound binding to a corresponding sensory receptor cell in our taste buds. Of these five tastes, only sweet, sour, and bitter are especially relevant to coffee. Salty and umami are tastes we don't generally associate with specialty coffee, and their presence is usually indicative of a mistake somewhere in the roasting or brewing process.

When tasting coffee, I like to imagine that sweet, sour, and bitter are in a love triangle. When the three are getting along, the coffee is delicious. But when sour and bitter are spending a little too much time together and sweet starts to get jealous, it can grow uncomfortable for everyone around them, and the coffee becomes decidedly less delicious.

In competition, scoring the flavor of coffee is in part based on accuracy of description, but also on the balance of the basic tastes. In practice, balancing the basic tastes is a three-way combination of selecting a coffee with an inherently balanced flavor profile, roasting this coffee in a way that lets the flavors shine, and properly extracting the flavors of the coffee during brewing. Poor handling of green coffee during processing or shipping, a bad roast, aging, or improper extraction will all lead to unbalanced acidity or bitterness, and a whole gamut of unpleasant flavors coming into play.

But this isn't to say that a balanced cup of coffee must be 33.33% sweet, 33.33% sour, and 33.33% bitter. Everyone involved in the chain of custody of a coffee has room to express creativity with the balance of flavors of a given coffee. No style is by its nature superior to another in anything other than a battle of personal preference. In fact, many styles have come and gone over the years, and currently, many coexist.

Preferred flavor balance and roast degree vary quite a bit culturally. Coffee aficionados in Norway, Japan, Ethiopia, and Brazil will all have different ideas of what makes a great cup of coffee. And of course, individuals from different cultures will have their own favorite styles, independent from the overarching style commonly available to them. The fact is that some people just like 'em a little zingier than others, and there's nothing wrong with that!

SWEETNESS

We have only one type of receptor for sweetness, and it can be triggered by many different chemical compounds. Sugars, as well as some alcohols, proteins, and artificial sweeteners can all bind to our eloquently named TAS1R receptors.[5]

Coffees with a great natural sweetness are delicious. In terms of our love triangle analogy, sweetness is the pretty flavor everyone gets along with, so even if it's talking over the other two, the relationship doesn't suffer. Consequently, finding the "sweet spot" when dialing in a coffee recipe often literally amounts to working out the recipe where the sweetness expresses itself the best. That said, a coffee with remarkably high natural sweetness dominating the other two core flavors is not common.

Sweetness in coffee comes from simple carbohydrates, or sugars. Sugars that appear naturally in coffee include sucrose, fructose, glucose, and galactose, with the sweetest being sucrose and fructose. The amount of sugar present in green coffee is dependent on many factors, including most importantly ripeness, as well as varietal or cultivar, growing conditions, and processing. [6]

Roasters and baristas cannot create sweetness, but they can do their best to make sure it isn't lost. Though these techniques are outside the scope of this book, the roaster who carefully degrade as little as possible, and the barista who nails their brewing recipe at that fine line before over-extraction creates an unbalanced bitterness will reap the reward of sweetness as well.

ACIDITY

Our sour taste receptor protein is called OTOP1. Our body recognizes acidity as a sour taste when hydrogen ions (H+) pass over an OTOP1 protein in our taste cells, triggering an electrical current. OTOP1 is called an ion channel. [7]

When the three basic tastes are balanced, acidity brings fruit to the table, and some of the most delicious coffees have a very present and unique acidity. While acidity is certainly the most interesting member of the love triangle, it also has the strongest personality of the three basic tastes, and it can quickly turn into an unhealthy relationship when acidity is in charge. An "unsupported acidity" is a very negative quality, since it results in a sour and unpleasant cup.

Overwhelming sourness elicits a strong biological response, as salivary glands jump into overdrive to try and dilute the acids so they don't kick our body's pH out of whack. If you've ever felt a painful, sharp sensation up near your ears when tasting something very sour, that's what that was. This experience can absolutely be triggered by an unbalanced coffee, as many baristas who've tasted especially under-extracted espresso while dialing in a recipe could tell you.

One of the big hurdles when dialing in a coffee recipe is the gradient of acidity, because without acidity, coffees have no vibrance or character, but with even a little too much, pleasing citrus can become painfully sour. When roasting a coffee or writing a brewing recipe, knowing where that line is takes care and precision.

Coffees that are grown at higher elevations tend to develop greater concentrations of acids, and the specific makeup of acids is dependent on the coffee's growing conditions.[8] There are several acids present in coffee, and they each contribute their own unique flavor, though some are easier to describe than others.

The acids present in coffee in any meaningful amount are:

Citric acid contributes the lemony acidity present in all citrus fruits.

Malic acid contributes the unmistakable acidity found in apples.

Acetic acid is the primary component in vinegar and that's what it tastes like. At lower concentrations, it contributes a winey acidity. To a degree, acetic acid is inversely proportional to sweetness, in that it's sucrose that brings about acetic acid during caramelization.

Phosphoric acid contributes to perceived acidity and imbues a hard-to-describe bright and sparkling note found notably in Kenyan coffees. Phosphoric acid is added to the "cola" style of soft drink and contributes to its characteristic flavor.

Tartaric acid contributes a very tart, sour acidity that is present in grapes and wine.

Lactic acid contributes the milky tang that is present in yogurt and sourdough bread. Lactic acid is formed during the fermentation stage of coffee processing.

Chlorogenic acid is the most bountiful acid present in green coffee, and it's responsible for perceived acidity and bitterness, as well as a lingering metallic taste in higher concentrations. During roasting, it breaks down into lactones, and further into phenylindanes, which significantly increase bitterness and astringency.

Coffee reaches its peak acidity during the roasting process around the moment called "first crack." This is the moment when moisture content within the beans changes to gas, creating an audible pop as the pressure busts out. After first crack, the acidity will start to decline. A skilled roaster will find a point where the acids are enhancing, not overpowering, the cup. Because acids are dissolved early in the brewing process, a good barista will focus on fully extracting their brew, allowing those acids to be diluted and balanced by other flavors that extract more slowly.

BITTERNESS

We have forty-three bitter receptors, called TAS2R proteins. Our bitter taste reception is there to help protect us from being poisoned, and simply put, we have a lot of different receptors with overlapping areas of coverage for a host of compounds because there have been many, many ways for us to poison ourselves over the course of human evolution. This makes us very attuned to bitterness.[9]

There are a few schools of thought in regard to bitterness in coffee. Some work to eliminate it completely. Some think it is what defines coffee, and they relish it. I think it ought to exist in harmony and bring out the best in its partners sweetness and acidity. In the love triangle, I think bitterness is like the distinguished-but-ugly one who makes the other two look better when they're all standing together—though bitterness can easily hog all the attention, too.

Bitterness in coffee comes from a variety of different places. Coffee is rich in polyphenols like chlorogenic acids, caffeine, diterpenes, and trigonelline. Caffeine, diterpenes, and trigonelline contribute to coffee's bitterness, and while chlorogenic acid itself is not bitter, its bitterness potential is realized throughout the roasting process as it is broken down into bitter chlorogenic acid lactones. These lactones are broken down further into phenylindanes, becoming increasingly bitter. Melanoidins produced during the Maillard reaction over the course of the roasting process contribute to bitterness, as well.

It's easy for roasters and baristas to make an unbelievably bitter coffee. Everyone has seen that shiny, charcoal-looking coffee that tastes how it looks. Many have experienced poorly prepared brews or espressos as well, where localized over-extraction (a.k.a. channeling) led to an overwhelming expression of bitterness in the cup. Avoiding excessively dark roasting or channeled brews, however, is theoretically a far simpler task than learning how to tread the gradient of acidity or accentuating sweetness.

AROMA

Recognizing the basic tastes is very easy, despite a few small confusions. Everyone can tell the difference between sweet and bitter, but sometimes bitter and sour can be confused for one another in a particularly concentrated espresso, for instance. We can confuse "very hot" for "bitter" as well. All in all, though, everyone should agree the basic tastes are easy. Lemons are sour, sugar is sweet, unsweetened chocolate is bitter. The real complication comes when we add in the other half of the equation, volatile aromatic compounds, or aroma.

We have around 400 different aroma receptors in different zones of our olfactory epithelium. The ones closest to our face encounter aromatic compounds we take in orthonasally first, while the ones closer to the back of our throat encounter compounds we take in retronasally. The receptors at the front of our nose are actually ones we share with fish (and our ancient aquatic common ancestor). Because of this, they're attuned to water-soluble compounds, which makes them excellent at detecting all those water-soluble compounds we work so hard to extract in coffee. It's also of note that retronasal olfaction is less effective with water-soluble compounds because they might be dissolved within our nose before they reach the appropriate receptor. [10]This is why it's advisable to take a breath in through the mouth after swallowing, expelling it deliberately through the nose, to improve your chances of experiencing all the aromatic compounds in combination with taste.

As I mentioned earlier, there are more than 1,000 different aromatic compounds present in coffee.[11] Volatile aromatic compounds develop in different ways in green coffees, depending on variety, terroir, ripeness, and processing. But green coffee aromatics aren't what we perceive so strongly when we brew coffee, many of those powerful aromatics are developed during the roasting process as the makeup of the green coffee is radically changed.

An array of complex chemical reactions and events occur during the roasting process which lead to the development of volatile aromatic compounds, notably, caramelization and Maillard reactions. After roasting, aromas are trapped within the roasted beans, but they do gradually escape through a process known as degassing. This is why old coffee will lack aroma and taste dull and stale, as its aroma has long since vacated the premises.

The aromas in fresh coffee are released on grinding and brewing with hot water. It's this release that can quickly fill a room and raise the sleeping from their beds. Later in this chapter, I will detail each of these 1,000 aromatic compounds and their attributes, along with handy memorization techniques.

Just kidding! There are too many volatile aromatic compounds for it to be practical to list them all with any meaningful detail in the context of a book like this (the book Coffee Flavor Chemistry by Ivon Flament does just this, if you want to take the deep dive).

There is, however, a much more digestible small group, around 5% of the total volatile aromatics, which we can separate from the larger mass because they have a lower "odor threshold," meaning they are distinctly perceptible, or especially "odiferous." The group can be further broken down into compounds that are thought to be essential to coffee aroma.[12]

This doesn't mean that all those other aromatic compounds are inconsequential to a particular coffee's flavor profile. You wish it was that simple! Compounds that are below the human odor threshold have their own part to play as well. Despite their "imperceptibility," compounds below the odor threshold have been found to significantly impact our perception of other aspects of a coffee—enhancing perception of sweetness, for instance[13] All those lower threshold compounds play an important part in each coffee's unique flavor profile, and that's how we're able to find more tasting notes than those that make up the description of the most odiferous ones.

But that aside, the compounds I really want to focus on are the ones that have notable appearances outside of coffee, or which we might have (or be able to develop) a frame of reference for, so we can learn to pick them out.

Each aromatic compound has a different polarity, those with a higher polarity are extracted more efficiently over the course of a brew. Those compounds with lower polarity extract more slowly and are extracted best with higher temperatures.[14] This is why low temperature brewing methods like "cold-brew" miss out on aromatics. Even an only somewhat lower brewing temperature due to thermal exchange between the brewing water and a cold ceramic brewer will result in missed aromatic content. You can find out how polar a compound is by looking at its boiling point. Compounds with higher boiling points are less polar, and, to reiterate, extract more slowly.

The fact that we have different aromatic compounds reaching their maximum concentration and dissipating at different rates over the course of a brew[15] really drives home the point that the flavor of coffee is constantly changing. It's not as simple as saying your coffee smells lemony. The combination of aromatics that smelled lemony to start with might change over the course of the brew to elicit a totally different association further down the line. To get a good picture of a particular coffee, you've got to spend time to experience the evolution of the cup.[16]

Depending on their solubility, different odorants will be more perceptible depending on the way they enter our system, with more soluble compounds being more perceptible orthonasally and less soluble compounds being more perceptible retronasally. This isn't to say that compounds in higher concentration won't be perceptible both ways, though. The important takeaway is that we're going to have different experiences depending on the way we bring aromatic compounds into our olfactory system, with receptors registering compounds in different orders, so we need to be conscious and think critically about them both.

COFFEE AND SCIENCE

Chemists have historically used many different techniques to determine what the individual aromatic constituents of coffee are, including gas chromatography and mass spectrometry. Also known as gas-liquid partition chromatography, gas chromatography uses a carrier gas, like helium, to carry the individual constituents through the system as they vaporize.

To determine the sensory aspects of compounds and their odor thresholds, the exit of the gas chromatograph will employ an incredibly complex and advanced sensor, THOS. THOS is an acronym I've created for The Human Olfactory System, which is a remarkable tool! Panels of real live humans will sit at the chromatograph exhaust and do things like hold down a button as long as they can perceive specific smells. I think this sounds like a lot of fun, but maybe that's just me.

Using techniques like these, scientists have come up with over one thousand compounds present in roasted coffee, but simply having a list of these compounds doesn't mean we know how to recreate coffee in a lab, although that won't stop people from trying. The meaningful advances to the coffee industry here come from the potential for chemical analysis of coffee to isolate those characteristics which make exceptional coffees exceptional. If these qualities are isolated, and the reasons for their occurrence are discovered, this information can be passed back to farmers who can use it to their advantage to produce better coffee. Everyone wins in that scenario.

World Coffee Research is a nonprofit agricultural research organization doing exactly this type of work in the area of genetic improvement of cup quality. They're looking for ways to get repeatable high-quality results while also maintaining resistance to diseases like La Roya (a.k.a. coffee leaf rust), a disease with the potential to completely devastate a farmer's hard work. The purpose of the organization is to get those developments back in the hands of producers and it's this type of work that is critical for the future of the industry. The team at WCR is doing the work to isolate these exceptional characteristics in the cup and trace them back to their origins. As an example, they have identified the presence of the aromatic compound limonene in coffee as a signifier of super-specialty-grade beans, and now they're looking for genetic markers that lead to its formation.[17]

Using modern technologies and science in combination with sensory skills to keep moving the industry forward is very exciting; this is the cutting edge. It's also an area I don't think many coffee professionals think about as they're working on their tasting skills. What I mean is, the end of the road for coffee tasting isn't necessarily a role as a green coffee buyer. There are many different potential avenues for someone with well-honed skills and a passion for the sensory aspects of coffee.

AROMATIC COMPOUNDS

The compounds listed in the following section are organized in the order in which they are extracted, based on their polarity, which I've ascertained by locating their boiling point.[18] This area of research is not widely publicized, so certain bits of information I'd love to be able to list here, such as the rate that all these compounds dissipate, are not frequently available in the research areas I have access to. Solubility is listed at room temperature of 25 °C (77°F), and just to clarify, the higher the g/L, the more soluble a substance is.

Diacetyl (2,3-butanedione)

Boiling point: 87°C

Solubility: 200 g/L @ 25 °C

This "buttery" type diketone compound has the flavor descriptors "sweet, creamy, pungent, caramelly." Diacetyl is the product of fermentation and is found naturally in cultured butter and sour cream, where it goes hand in hand with lactic acid. It can be found naturally in beers and especially buttery wines like chardonnay. It is also used in artificial butter flavorings.[19] Diacetyl dissipates quickly after reaching its maximum intensity.

Acetylpropionyl (2,3-pentanedione)

Boiling point: 108°C

Solubility: 60 g/L @ 25 °C

This "buttery" type diketone compound has odor descriptions of "pungent, sweet, buttery, creamy, caramelly, nutty, cheesy." Acetylpropionyl is a byproduct of fermentation and is found naturally occurring, among other things, in butter, bread, milk, and yogurt. It tends to appear alongside diacetyl, but the odor threshold is higher, making it more difficult to perceive. Acetylpropionol does not dissipate as fast over the course of the brew, leading me to the hypothesis that buttery, creamy aromas perceived later on in a brew's lifetime might be attributed to it instead of diacetyl.

Prenyl Mercaptan (3-Methyl-2-buten-1-thiol)

Boiling point: 128°C

Solubility: 0.718 g/L @ 25 °C

This "sulfurous" odor type alkylthiol compound has generally unpleasant sounding descriptors: "smoky, leek, onion, skunk." If you've ever experienced a skunked beer (beer spoiled due to light exposure), this is the compound responsible. Beer tasters are taught to look for the aroma of "skunk and freshly brewed coffee" when training to recognize light-struck beer.

Furfuryl Mercaptan (2-Furfurylthiol)

Boiling point: 155°C

Solubility: 2.216 g/L @ 25 °C

This "coffee" type compound is easy to pick out because it smells like "roasted coffee". It's found most notably in roasted coffee and has been determined to be coffee's most odor active compound.

Methional (3-Methylsulfanylpropanal)

Boiling point: 165°C

Solubility: 50.55 g/L @ 25 °C

This "vegetable" type compound smells like potatoes. With notes of "musty, tomato, brothy, vegetable, cheesy," it's found most notably in potato chips, with that characteristic aroma as you open the bag.

Limonene (1-Methyl-4-(prop-1-en-2-yl)cyclohex-1-ene)

Boiling point: 176°C

Solubility: 0.0138 g/L @ 25 °C

This "citrus" type compound smells like "orange, fresh, and sweet" and is found notably in citrus rinds. This compound has been identified as a marker for high quality in specialty coffee by World Coffee Research.21

Cocoa Pyrazine (2-Ethyl-3,5-dimethylpyrazine)

Boiling point: 180°C

Solubility: 1.473 g/L @ 25 °C

This "nutty" type compound has an aroma of "burnt almond, roasted, nutty, and coffee." It's found most notably in coffee, as well as in raw asparagus, wheat bread, roasted meats, and black tea, among other things.

Sotolon (3-Hydroxy-4,5-dimethylfuran-2(5H)-one)

Boiling point: 184°C

Solubility: 222.8 g/L @ 25 °C

This "caramelic" type compound has an aroma of "sweet, maple, sugar, burnt sugar." Sotolon, also called caramel furanone, is a primary odorant in fenugreek, and at high concentrations smells like curry. At lower concentrations, it smells very much like maple syrup. It is used in imitation maple syrup.

Bean Pyrazine (2-Isopropyl-3-methoxypyrazine)

Boiling point: 189°C

Solubility: 0.6986 g/L @ 25 °C

This "earthy" type compound contributes an aroma of "beany, chocolatey, potato." This is actually the compound responsible for the flavor of the infamous "potato defect" in African coffees. For those who aren't familiar, the potato defect can fill a room with an overpowering dirt/potato smell with the grinding of even one bean. While the aroma of methional is associated with a more or less pleasant potato-ness, bean pyrazine is remarkably unappealing at high concentrations.[20]

Linalool (3,7-Dimethyl-1,6-octadien-3-ol)

Boiling point: 194°C

Solubility: 1.589 g/L @ 25 °C

This "floral" type compound has an aroma of "citrus, floral, sweet, blueberry." It is found notably in blueberries. Linalool is much more prevalent in natural-processed coffees than washed coffees. If you've ever had a natural that was a real "blueberry bomb", linalool had something to do with it.

Guaiacol (2-Methoxyphenol)

Boiling point: 205°C

Solubility: 7.226 g/L @ 25 °C

This "phenolic" odor type compound has a description of "smoky, spicy, bacon, vanilla, woody." This aromatic compound was isolated in guaiacum, which is a flowering plant native to the tropics in the Americas. As a very interesting (though not relevant to tasting) tidbit, guaiacum was the first word in the English language of American origin[21], and Guaiacum officinale is the national flower of Jamaica. Guaiacol is a key aroma component in whisky, where it brings the smoky spiciness we associate especially with Islay Scotch whisky.

Bell Pepper Pyrazine (2-isobutyl-3-methoxypyrazine)

Boiling point: 214°C

Solubility: 0.2296 g/L @ 25 °C

This "green" odor type compound smells like green peppers, and is found notably in all peppers, such as bell peppers, contributing to that distinctive pepper smell.

Furaneol (4-Hydroxy-2,5-dimethyl-3-furanone)

Boiling point: 215°C

Solubility: 18.5 g/L @ 25 °C

This "caramelic" type compound has an aroma of "sweet, caramel, fruity, cooked pineapple, strawberry." Furaneol, also known as strawberry furanone, is found in many fruits, like strawberry and pineapple.

4VG (4-Vinylguaiacol)

Boiling point: 224°C

Solubility: 0.926 g/L @ 25 °C

This "woody" type compound has an odor description of "sweet, spicy, clove-like." 4VG is a large contributor to the distinctive aroma of buckwheat, and it's this compound that gives Bavarian Weissbier its clove-like flavors.[22] In high concentrations, it could contribute to a medicinal quality.

4EG (4-Ethyl Guaiacol)

Boiling point: 235°C

Solubility: 0.6938 g/L @ 25 °C

This "spicy" type compound has an aroma of "spicy, smoky, bacon, phenolic, clove." Ethyl guaiacol can be found as a byproduct of Brettanomyces yeast, which is the thing that brings that unique wild flavor to Belgian style beers like lambics, saisons, and farmhouse ales.[23] It can also be found in green tea, red wine, and shoyu (soy sauce).

Shoyu Furanone (5-Ethyl-4-hydroxy- 2-methyl-3(2H)-furanone)

Boiling point: 248°C

Solubility: 6.178 g/L @ 25 °C

This "caramelic" odor type compound has an odor description of "sweet, caramelly, bready, maple sugar, brown sugar, burnt." It has been isolated as a major component of shoyu. [24]

Abhexon (5-Ethyl-3-hydroxy-4-methyl-2(5H)-furanone)

Boiling point: 272°C

Solubility: 74.390 g/L @ 25 °C

This "caramelic" type compound has an aroma of "sweet, fruity, maple, fenugreek, chicory, praline, butterscotch." Though it takes a while to extract, maple furanone is a long lasting aromatic, actually one of the most powerful flavor chemicals known to science.[25]Abhexon, also known as Maple Furanone, is similar in aroma profile to sotolon, though extracting slower and lasting longer. It has a more pronounced flavor of maple than sotolon. Abhexon naturally occurs in shoyu.

Beta Damascenone ((E)-1-(2,6,6-Trimethyl-1-cyclohexa-1,3-di- enyl)but-2-en-1-one)

Boiling point: 274°C

Solubility: .01248 g/L @ 25 °C

This is part of a group of chemical compounds called "rose ketones." It is a major contributor to the aroma of roses, as well as a primary odorant in Kentucky Bourbon[26]. It is classified as having a "fruity" odor type and descriptor words of "apple, rose, honey, tobacco, and sweet." [27]

Vanillin (4-Hydroxy-3-methoxybenzaldehyde)

Boiling point: 285°C

Solubility: 6.875 g/L @ 25 °C

I guarantee you can guess this one. This "vanilla" type compound smells like—yep, you got it—vanilla, and is the primary component in vanilla extract.

PUTTING IT ALL TOGETHER

Especially once you start looking at aromatics, breaking a coffee down into its constituent parts is no simple task. That said, looking at those individual constituents on their own is not so daunting. With practice, identifying individual acids and aromatics is undeniably within the limits of the human senses, and once they can be identified, they can be utilized. A whole world of flavor combinations opens up to those who are willing to delve deep enough.

3. The Sensory Experience

AROMATIC BALANCE AND PERCEPTION

While I was researching aromatic compounds, I found that scientific literature relating to coffee aroma can use pretty boring and unpleasant sounding words to describe smells. Scientists have a rigorous system to determine their lexicon, but their language doesn't exactly make you want to taste the stuff they're describing. Even though we know that coffee is delicious, sensory science word choice and customer-facing retail word choice are vastly different. When I looked at the work of perfumers and the flavor industry, I found much more descriptive and flowery vocabulary talking about the same compounds. These words are more along the lines of the type of language that is appropriate when talking with guests about specialty-grade coffee.

In addition to different contexts necessitating different word choice, differences in aromatic balance might lead to some of those unpleasant sounding words. Robusta, for instance, contains higher concentrations of phenols and pyrazines, which impart negative qualities in high concentrations.[28] Volatile aromatic compounds can give us wildly different impressions depending on their concentrations. The same way that a balance of the basic flavors leads to a pleasing cup and an imbalance could lead to a sour and unpleasant cup, volatile aromatics show their best side in balance as well. This is how 4VG can bring that delightful clove quality to Bavarian Weissbier, but too much would be considered an "off" note, and make things kind of unappetizing and chemical/medicinal, just like it does in Robusta coffees. But even among Arabica varieties, there's a reason some coffees perform better on the cupping table than others; it's their balance of tastes and aromatics. I wonder if we'd get some more pleasant word choice from scientists if they were performing chemical analyses on well-roasted 90+ point coffees prepared by a world-class barista.

Volatile aromatics combine together to create odor objects. Our brain interprets odor objects on their own when we take in smells orthonasally, but when we experience them retronasally we combine them with what we're tasting. If you've ever had a peaty Islay Scotch whisky, you'll know that the smoky smelling compound guaiacol is perceptible when you take a whiff, but try taking a sip with your nose plugged, then unplug after you swallow. The smoky character disappears completely, then reappears when you unplug your nose. Because of the alcohol, there's a bit of a nip to the flush of air going through your nose, giving you a very vivid sense of the way those odorants are entering your nasal passageway. Despite being fully cognizant that the smokiness is something that exists in your nose, and even experiencing sensation in your nose, we still experience it simultaneously in our mouth as one combined taste. Plugging and unplugging of the nose can be a good way to separate the basic tastes from the aromas when we're trying to pinpoint flavors we recognize while cupping coffee.

An important thing to note when considering human perception of taste and aroma is that from individual to individual, our perceptions will differ a good deal. You may have heard the term "super-taster"—someone who is very sensitive to taste sensations. What's mildly bitter to me might be extremely bitter to them. There's really a range of sensitivity to taste and aroma in humans, with genetics leading to different people falling at different places along the gradient.

In addition to our general sensitivity, some people actually have more working flavor and odor receptors than others. This is the reason only some people find cilantro to have a weird, soapy taste, and it's not limited to our perception of cilantro. The evidence suggests that everyone has their own unique way of perceiving flavor. If you can't taste something that someone else can in a cup of coffee, it may not simply be because you lack experience; that taste just might not be in the cards for you. By the same token, you could excel at tasting certain things that another person will not taste at all. By all accounts, with any two given people, this will be the case. I think this is critical to keep in mind when sharing a tasting experience with someone else. The fact that your tasting partner doesn't pick up on the orange creamsicle flavor you so distinctly taste doesn't necessarily mean that they're a noob or a poser, or that you're crazy for suggesting it.

DESCRIBING TASTE

There are a number of flavor-complex liquids that share common aromatic compounds with roasted coffee. Whiskey, beer, wine, brandies, even soy sauce and other fermented products all have very complex flavor profiles that share a lot in common with coffee. These specialty products all have their own schools of thought and disciplines related to tasting, independent of coffee, and there's a lot to be learned from the methods and language used by specialists in other areas.

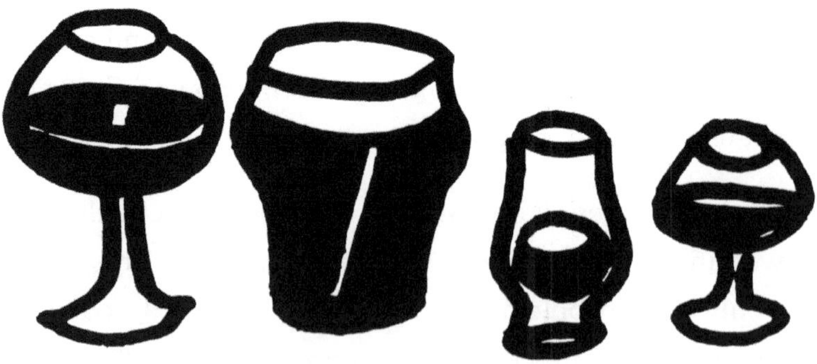

For instance, in other industries, a visual analysis of the liquid is standard practice. Beer, wine, and spirits are all tasted in clear glass to facilitate evaluation of clarity and color, and wine and spirits are swirled as part of the visual analysis as well to facilitate evaluation of the texture by watching how the liquid clings and drips down the sides of the glass. This isn't common practice with brewed coffee because the cupping for mat through which coffee is evaluated is not particularly conducive to visual evaluation, but this doesn't mean it's impossible. Simply scooping a few spoonfuls from the cupping bowl into a clear glass like a brandy snifter makes a visual analysis possible.

The art of balancing aromas is also something perfumers do incredibly well. There's a lot we can learn about deciphering coffee's aroma from the way perfumers build smells. There's a cavernous rabbit hole of online resources to dive down about perfumery, but I think something really important we can glean right on the surface level is how perfumers break smells down: head, heart, and base. The head of the fragrance is the note that hits you right off the bat. The heart of the fragrance is the most dominant; it comes in after the head and sticks with you. The base is what's lingering under it all and will stick around the longest. Try thinking about the aroma of coffee with this framework, it might help you to notice some things you've been missing.

The specific words we choose to describe taste are also a product of our own native language. It's interesting how different groups use different words to talk about the same concept.

Our language is what gives a framework for our thoughts. This should be readily apparent to everyone, as we think in our native language. Anyone who has learned a second language, especially one with a very different syntax from their native language, will know that it might not always be possible to express precise words or ideas from their native language or vice versa. For example, that special glee you experience when someone else hurts themselves or screws up can be quickly expressed by the German speaker with the word "schadenfreude." In English, we borrow the German word, but many English speakers don't know it. For them, the concept of schadenfreude can't be neatly and concisely parceled. This phenomenon is even more pronounced between very different languages, such as Mandarin and English. This is the type of thing that's happening when we're learning to put a name to different flavors and communicate them to someone else.

Two different coffees compared side by side might have a wildly different flavor profile, which the English language hasn't given us the means to convey. Because of this, simply saying that they each taste like "coffee" is inadequate. Giving an array of specific flavor notes isn't really adequate either. Even though my own personal sensory memory might make a strong connection between a black honey-processed gesha variety coffee from Finca Chelin in Mexico and those strawberry candies my great-grandma had in a dish on the table when I visited her once as a three-year-old, this meaning is only accessible to me. So how do I communicate this abstract concept to someone with a different sensory memory than I have? How do we know that what we taste as "grapefruit" is the same as what someone else will taste as "grapefruit" if we can't even be certain they've ever tried grapefruit?

There are resources that exist for the specific purpose of bringing a common language to coffee tasting. The World Coffee Research Sensory Lexicon and the related SCA Coffee Taster's

Flavor Wheel are two such resources available for free online. The Flavor Wheel is a pie chart filled with different flavors that might be present in brewed coffee.

The lexicon is a repeatable way of recreating those flavors using easy access items. For example, to illustrate grapefruit flavor with an intensity of 11, all we have to do is serve Ocean Spray brand 100% white grapefruit juice. This way, we know someone familiar with the lexicon ought to know exactly what we mean when we say "grapefruit." The foremost benefit of the lexicon is to get industry professionals calibrated with each other, that way, when a farmer in Colombia and a green coffee buyer in the US want to talk about flavor, for example, they have a shared vocabulary that all parties understand.

These tools are very valuable, but they only solve the problem for parties who are familiar with the resources. In the situation where a barista and a guest are trying to come to an understanding about what a specific coffee is about to taste like, the sensory lexicon is less helpful, especially considering some of the flavor references are not simple to obtain, or are very expensive, and the likelihood that a non-industry individual will be familiar with the sensory lexicon is very low.

DESCRIBING THE TASTE OF COFFEE

What the barista needs is some way to find out the common sensory language they share with their guest. Simply saying this coffee has notes of "muscovado, lychee, jasmine, and honeydew" is not enough. Not only are these four words not an accurate representation of what the coffee actually tastes like (they're more like saying, "I think this super complex flavor shares some qualities with 'muscovado, lychee, jasmine, and honeydew'"), but if you're trying to convey this complex flavor to someone who doesn't know what muscovado is, hasn't tried lychee, could barely differentiate jasmine from any other flower, and is really thinking of cantaloupe when you say honeydew, it's like trying to put a square peg in a round hole. The barista needs a quick way to establish a shared vocabulary to transfer this imperfect bit of abstract data between their brains.

Another problem of semantics related to tasting is that even though our sensory memory might be shouting at us that the flavor we're tasting in a particular coffee is "blueberry," that flavor is not blueberry. It's a specific mix of volatile aromatics, and basic tastes that remind us of what we remember blueberries tasting like. Some people say that alligator tastes like chicken, but that's just because they're much more familiar with the flavor of chicken than they are with the flavor of alligator. Someone who eats alligator for breakfast, lunch, and dinner might say that chicken tastes a lot like alligator.

Bear with me here: Plato theorized a realm of perfect forms. On Earth, there's no such thing as a perfectly straight line, but, Plato speculated, in the Platonic Realm, the perfectly straight line does exist, and that's where our idea of the straight line, or the perfect sphere or triangle is projected from. We have this idea of what blueberries taste like which comes from our sensory memory. But the concept of what it means to be a blueberry, the idea of "blueberriness" is tied to many more abstract concepts than the bit of data we have stored.

Blueberries are spherical, they're blue, and they have a mix of textures from the skin, flesh, and seeds. They have a distinct blueberry flavor. We have an image in our mind of "a blueberry," which I think is closer to what might exist in the Platonic realm than the real thing. In reality, blueberries can be quite weirdly shaped. They have a range of colors and flavors depending on ripeness, cultivar, and just the individual blueberry. Some blueberries are red! Of these abstract attributes that blueberries possess, ("sphere-ness," "blue-ness," etc.) what they actually share in common with coffee is that ripe blueberries have, among other things, sugars, citric acid, polyphenols, and the aromatic compounds linalool, hexanal, limonene, 2,4-hexadienal, cucumber aldehyde, and butyl acetate. But they also contain a bunch of stuff that coffee does not, and without those things, they would definitely not be blueberries.

What I'm really trying to say here is that we can say that things taste like other things, but we're not learning anything unless we uncover why this is so. The coffee producer, roaster, or barista who learns why their coffees taste the way they do can come up with quick and easily digestible ways to introduce new flavor concepts and language. In short, they can talk about flavor without sounding like a bullshit artist. In the next section, we'll go over a bunch of different real world things that you can taste that share volatile aromatics or specific tastes with coffee, so the next time you say that a coffee has "notes" of this or that, you'll be able to say why, too.

SENSORY SIBLINGS: APPROACHES TO PALATE EXPANSION

There are many ways to broaden one's palate of flavors. There are products available to coffee professionals to help expand their sensory skill-sets, such as the Le Nez du Café aroma kit and FlavorActiV flavor capsules. While these kits are simple and effective to a degree, in my opinion, they're priced out of range of individuals and small businesses. My experience with these kits is that they are very educational but not especially fun or delicious in the way that eating real fruit is, for instance.

On the other end of the spectrum from these very specific coffee sensory kits, there's the somewhat directionless approach of actively and thoughtfully tasting throughout your everyday life. I've found this to be widely encouraged within the industry, and while there is some value in this approach, simply tasting many random things is to palate expansion what the infinite monkeys at the typewriter strategy is for writing a novel. Eventually you'll get there, but you'll get there much, much faster if you have structure.

While this isn't strictly necessary, I think it's important to set a deliberate environment and enter a specific mindset to get the most out of tasting. I believe a combination of structured rigor and fun reaps the greatest reward. Clutter is distracting, so make sure to tidy up, and ideally clear the table. You'll want to keep a notebook to write down your thoughts and takeaways, and be diligent about writing in it. Remember that this is really the same sort of mental process as studying for school, but instead of absorbing facts or equations, we're absorbing flavors.

I think it's important to taste things one at a time, a methodical deep-dive down one flavor pathway is much more useful for your brain than a brute force bombardment of variety, as the brain forges connections based on repetition. Taking it slow also helps to cushion the monetary hit of actually buying all these different things to taste. It is very helpful to have others on board if the cost of these exercises is an impediment for you.

It's also good to taste in a pair or group to better facilitate blind tasting, which is an indispensable part of your growth in the skill. A true blind tasting involves one person doing the setup and sacrificing their ability to take part in the "blind" experience. Ideally, this person would buy the samples as well, and the others taking part in the tasting wouldn't even know what was on the table until they dove in. This is certainly not always practical, however. An easy way to make a blind tasting with two people is to have one person set up the samples, then the second mix them up after they're covered.

If you don't have a partner, you can still make an approximation of a blind tasting. Put all your samples in their own covered container, labeled on the bottom. They should be cut or broken into small enough pieces that you can use a small spoon to move them to your mouth without looking.

Close your eyes and mix them up on the table until you don't remember which is which (time to break out the lazy Susan). Then label them A, B, C, etc. so you have some name to reference in your notes before you reveal which is which.

Start by trying each one in a series, without thinking too hard. Note your first impressions. Now try each one, smelling first, then tasting, and really think about what their defining characteristics are. Write those down. If you tried one at random, could you pick out which it was by taste alone? How about by smell alone? Reveal the names and taste again.

Below, I'm going to break down a fair number of foods and beverages you might reasonably find as a "tasting note" in coffee. This is because these items all share a notable amount of chemical compounds with coffee.

A turning point in my coffee education was listening to a talk at the SCAA Symposium by Intelligentsia founder Doug Zell, in which he talked about pairing coffee with food. He included some recipes, including a barbecue sauce I still use to this day. So if you're wondering what to do with leftovers, take the opportunity to experiment with flavor pairings based on what you've learned and see what you come up with!

If you're ready to begin, we'll start with a fun and easy one.

APPLE

Apple is the fruit we associate most strongly with malic acidity, which is one of the most common acids in coffee. We're starting with apple on our palate expansion journey because, to those outside the coffee industry, apple is definitely not the flavor they'd call out when describing what coffee tastes like. In reality, though, it is very common and very easy to recognize. Some of the most delicious, competition-level coffees I've had the privilege to try have had an astonishing sweetness and apple flavor. Once you're attuned to how malic acidity in apples feels on your tongue, you'll start to recognize that sensation when tasting coffee as well.

In addition to malic acid, apples also share ethyl hexanoate, beta damascenone, 1-hexanol, 2-hexenal, and butyl acetate with coffee.

You can tell apples are ripe when they are firm and crisp. If an apple is bruised or wrinkly or has too much give when you squeeze it, it's past its prime and might have a mealy texture and loss of flavor.

To really get the idea behind malic acid, try a green cooking apple (like a Granny Smith). A good coffee balances the acidity with sweetness, so try a sweeter apple as well (like a Fuji or Honeycrisp). Round it out with a fruit from the same family (Pome fruits), a pear. Pome fruits are a subfamily of roses, beta-damascenone, a major contributor to the aroma of roses, is found in apples as well and can be brought to the forefront by stewing. In addition to eating them raw, try stewing as well as pan-frying some apples to observe the impact of cooking and the Maillard reaction on the aroma.

CITRUS

Citrus fruits are the poster boy for citric acid. Lemons and limes are made up of as much as 8% citric acid.[29] Some aromatic compounds that citrus fruits share with coffee are limonene and linalool. Interestingly, limonene has been named as an identifying factor of coffee quality, meaning high quality specialty coffees are likely to have a notable presence of limonene.[30] The meat of citrus fruits, or the pulp, doesn't contain many aromatics. The aromatic content of citrus fruit is all jammed into the rind, or zest.

To really get the idea of citric acid, squeeze some lemon into a glass of water and taste that. I'd avoid tasting straight up lemons on their own if you don't want to burn out your palate.

To wrap your head around the aromatics, zest the fruits and smell them, and to get the flavor experience, make infusions of hot water and zest to taste instead of tasting the pulp. It's important to separate citric acid from each fruit's defining aromatic profile.

Try smelling the zest and tasting zest infusions of every citrus fruit you can get your hands on. Different types of oranges, regular and Meyer lemons, limes and key limes, grapefruit, mandarins, kumquats, and pomelos.

In this same category, I'd recommend smelling and tasting Earl Grey tea, a black tea flavored with oil of bergamot, an essential oil high in linalool and limonene.

BERRIES

We can break berries up into three branches: strawberries are their own branch called Fragaria, raspberries and blackberries belong to the family Rubus, and finally, blueberries and cranberries belong to Vaccinium. Both Fragaria and Rubus are related to roses, while Vaccinium are heathers.

While we group berries together, they're all pretty different. Different berries will highlight different acids and have varying sweetness and diverse aromatic makeup, though they do share some common compounds, like linalool.

Strawberries notably share citric acid, furaneol, linalool, as well as ethyl butanoate (a piney, banana, and pineappley compound) and methyl butanoate (a distinctly fruity, somewhat peachy aromatic) with coffee.

Raspberries share citric acid, beta damascenone, furaneol,

limonene, linalool, and caryophyllene (a woody, spicy compound) with coffee. Notably, the number one aromatic contributing to raspberry aroma, raspberry ketone, is not present in coffee.

Blackberries notably share malic acid, furaneol, linalool, caryophyllene, 2-heptanone (a fresh-lemony-floral compound), and 2-heptanol (a fresh, green floral, fruity compound) with coffee.

Blueberries notably share quite a lot with coffee: citric acid, linalool, limonene, 2,4-hexadienal (a green, fatty, fruity compound), cucumber aldehyde (a cucumber, green, fruity, and perfumy compound), 3-octanone (a herbaceous-fruity compound similar to lavender oil) and butyl acetate (a fruity ripe- pear type compound).

Cranberries notably share quinic, malic, and citric acid, as well as linalool, limonene, 3-octanone, and benzaldehyde (an aromatic with sweet, crushed bitter almond qualities) with coffee.

I'd recommend smelling and tasting both cut raw berries and cooked berries to get the full picture here.

CHOCOLATE

Chocolate is a very common flavor descriptor in coffee, to the point that it is maybe more of a lazy crutch than a truly descriptive word. The term "baker's chocolate" is a common

positive spin on the flavor that is simply "bitter," but chocolate really does have a distinct and relevant flavor to coffee that is much more complex than one bitter note. Cocoa contains more than 600 aromatic compounds. 3-methylbutanoic acid, furaneol (strawberry furanone), 2-ethyl-3,5-dimethylpyr azine (cocoa pyrazine), benzaldehyde, and linalool are a few common aromatics with coffee.

Dark chocolate is made by mixing cocoa butter with semi-solid cocoa and sugar. The addition of dried milk results in milk chocolate. Dairy brings with it a host of compounds that we'll cover in the next section.

Taste a range of chocolate bars. If possible, buy dark chocolate made with cocoa grown in different countries of origin, like some of the bars available from Askinosie or Dandelion Chocolate. Try unsweetened, bittersweet, and semi-sweet chocolate used for baking. Try different brands of milk chocolate, including Swiss, Belgian, or other European milk chocolate.

DAIRY

Dairy and coffee share a whole host of compounds in common, which is one of the reasons coffee and milk pair so well together. The dairy tasting note is often unrecognized but is exceedingly common. Lactic acid and diacetyl are two important compounds present in milk and coffee. They also share 2-propanone, 2-butanone, 2-pentanone, 2-heptanone, acetaldehyde, 1-octanol, hexyl methyl ketone, 1-heptanol, vanillin, 2-undecanone, and hexanoic acid, among many others.

Try raw milk if available, whole milk vs. cream, and observe lactic acid by tasting yogurts, sour cream, and buttermilk, and butter for that hit of diacetyl.

SPICE

I find the spice note I can pinpoint in coffee is most often anise-like. The primary aromatic compound in fennel and aniseed anethole, however, coffee does not share. That licoricy flavor present in fennel and other spices like anise, star anise and licorice is certainly a flavor note present in coffee. 4-methoxybenzaldehyde (anisaldehyde) hits that note and is indeed found in coffee as well as anise, fennel, star anise,

and licorice. Also in common we find limonene, linalool, and 1-isopropyl-4-methylbenzene. Eugenol is present in clove and cinnamon, as well as coffee and star anise. Vanilla shares the appropriately named compound vanillin with coffee.

Make mild hot water infusions of fennel, star anise, clove, cinnamon, and vanilla extract. Use freshly ground up whole spices and do a pinch of the spices steeped in a cup of water, fresh off the boil. Smell and taste these infusions.

GRAPES

There are thousands of different grape varieties; they can be divided into wine, juice, and table grapes. At the grocery store, the availability is usually limited to generic green and red table grapes. If you have a local farmer's market, there should be grapes available there that offer a little more variety to add breadth to your grape knowledge. In common with coffee, grapes contain malic acid, tartaric acid, sugars, 1-hexanol, 3-hexen-1-ol, ethyl acetate, 3-methylphenol, acetophenone, 4-hydroxynonanoic acid lactone.

Try red grapes, white grapes, black raisins, golden raisins. Try some distillations of grapes as well, Cognac, Armagnac or other grape-based brandy will have the essence of grapes without any acids (if you can get past the alcohol). Wines provide an excellent tasting experience, but perhaps a bit more complexity than is valuable in describing coffee flavor, as I'll touch on later.

The buttery flavor found notably in California chardonnays is produced by diacetyl, a byproduct of malolactic conversion, which is the breakdown of malic acid into lactic acid.[31] Diacetyl and lactic acid are both elements present in coffee, so wines like this are a great intro to these distinct flavors. Try the Josh Cellars or Kendall Jackson chardonnays for a great example of a buttery wine, but if you ask for a buttery chardonnay at your local wine purveyor they can steer you in the right direction as well. If you're tasting wines, you should have something to contrast, definitely try it next to a zingy, dry white like a sauvignon blanc or a European-style chardonnay, which won't have the same buttery-ness as its Californian cousin.

SUGARS AND SWEETS

Obviously sugars are sweet, but different sugary substances have their own identifying aromatic characteristics that help us easily tell them apart. In addition to sugars:

Caramel shares 5-hydroxymethylfurfural, maltol, guiacol, diacetyl. Furaneol, and vanillin with coffee.

Honey shares with coffee, 1-(2-furanyl)-ethanone, 2,3-butenediol, 3-hydroxy-2-butanone, linalool, 2-phenylethanol, and 4-methoxybenzaldehyde, among others.

Molasses shares dimethyl sulfide, furaneol, 2-methylbutanoic acid, 2-propanol, coumaran, 2,6-dimethoxyphenol, and propionic acid, among others, with coffee.

Maple syrup shares vanillin, methylpyrazine, 2,3-dimethylpyrazine, acetol, and furaneol, among others, with coffee.

Make mild hot water infusions of raw cane sugar, caramel, honey, molasses, and maple syrup. Smell and taste in a cupping format, as described later in this book.

NUTS

"Nutty" is another flavor descriptor which comes up more due to its familiarity than its applicability. But as with chocolate, it certainly has its place and moments of relevance, especially with some specificity.

Almonds share benzaldehyde, furaneol, and furfural with coffee.

Walnuts share hexanal and pentanal with coffee.

Peanuts share 2-isopropyl-3-methoxypyrazine with coffee. Pecans share 3-methylbutanal and 4-vinylphenol with coffee.

Hazelnuts share linalool, 2-methoxy-3,5-dimethylpyrazine, and 4-methylphenol with coffee.

Pick up raw, unsalted almonds, walnuts, peanuts, pecans and hazelnuts. Though you should reserve some raw nuts as well, toast some up in the oven, making sure they don't burn, as the aromatics will really come with Maillard reactions. Set up a little blind tasting and see if you can tell the difference between these raw and toasted nuts by smell or taste alone before revealing their identities.

STONE FRUITS

Stone fruits are those fruits with pits inside, like plums. You can tell stone fruits are ripe because their aromatics become apparent through the peel, and they have a bit of give. Stone fruits predominantly contain malic acid and share many similar aromatics with each other.

Peaches and nectarines share linalool, benzaldehyde, and 4-hydroxy pentanoic acid lactone with coffee.

Apricots and plums share -y-decalactone, hexyl acetate, and methyl 2-hydroxybenzoate with coffee.

Cherries share benzaldehyde, and benzyl alcohol with coffee.

TROPICAL FRUITS

Methyl hexanoate is present significantly across all tropical fruits, as well as in coffee. In addition to this:

Mangos share citric, malic, and tartaric acid, as well as ethyl 3-methylbutanoate with coffee.

Pineapples share citric and malic acid (more citric than malic), as well as furaneol with coffee.

Bananas share malic and citric acid (mostly malic), isoamyl acetate and isoamyl alcohol with coffee.

Passion fruits share citric acid, as well as 3-hydroxy-2-buta-none, 2-heptanol, ethyl hexanoate and methyl benzoate with coffee.

Coconuts share gamma nonalactone and 2-undecanone with coffee.

Papayas share citric and malic acid (in equal parts), linalool, decenal and 2-methylthiophene with coffee.

MISC.

Flowers – You can make tea with rose petals as well as rose hips, passion flower, hibiscus, chamomile, lavender, jasmine and a whole host of other flowers.

Fungi – Try different types of edible mushrooms, I highly recommend candy-cap mushrooms, as they have aromatics just like maple and are quite a trip (but not that kind of trip!). Make a mushroom tea with ground up dried mushrooms.

Melon – Melons have a striking aroma, which is easily detectable through the rind, especially when they're ripe. This is an uncommon, but desirable tasting note in coffee. In addition to sugars, melons share isobutyl acetate, 1-hexanol, isopentyl acetate, (E)-2-nonenal, and nonanal with coffee. Try watermel on, cantaloupe, and honeydew.

Maillard – The Maillard reaction [DC9]is hugely impactful on the flavor of coffee. This reaction is what's occurring when food is browned through cooking, like a chicken breast with that beautiful golden brown crust. Try some other stuff that has gone through the Maillard reaction: toast, toasted marshmallows, nicely seared steak, pork, or tofu for the vegetarian, etc. What do these things share in common with coffee?

OTHER FLAVOR-COMPLEX FOODSTUFFS

Beer, whiskey, wine, soy sauce, chocolate, and tea, among many other flavor complex things, have a surface level under- standing we can come to, but they also have a rabbit-hole you can dive down. Sommeliers, for instance, have dedicated their lives to the intricacies of wine. I think a good rule of thumb is: if the tasting note you're thinking of using is something that has its own system of tasting notes, this is a tasting note you're going to need to get more specific about. Is it "winey" or is it really a specific type of wine you are calling out? What is it that says "winey," a grape juicy flavor? A boozy fermentedness? Is it the tartaric acid? A dry tannic sensation in the mouthfeel?

It's always eye-opening to see the way experts in these other flavor complex specialty products work, so if you can get to a tasting event and listen to these experts talk and ask questions, it will always give you a different perspective. The craft beer scene especially is rife with coffee collaborations, and those aren't limited to the ubiquitous coffee stout. Collaborations are a great indication that there are similarities to be explored.

Part II: How to Taste Coffee

4. Cupping

Cup tasting, or cupping, is the industry standard method of preparing and evaluating coffee. Very simply, we let ground coffee and hot water sit together in a bowl, then we slurp it with a spoon and note how the flavor changes over time. As long as the cupping recipe, water chemistry, water temperature, and grind quality are the same, cupping a specific coffee in any location should yield identical results.

The cupping preparation makes it very easy to brew many different coffees at once without needing a whole host of brewing devices or having to brew one coffee after another, leaving them to cool at different rates. We use the cup tasting process as a way to mitigate the impact of brewing technique on our perception of the character of a coffee, especially when compared alongside other coffees.

There are many different reasons why one would cup coffee in a professional setting. Green coffee buyers will cup coffee to help them decide which coffees to buy. Roasters will cup coffee to help them dial in their roasting process and to facilitate quality control. The Alliance for Coffee Excellence tastes thousands of cups as part of the scoring for the Cup of Excellence Competition, a prestigious coffee auction highlighting some of the best coffee producers in the world. In coffee bars, baristas cup coffee to help choose which coffees to serve, write their recipes, and quality control.

Outside of professional settings, any individual might cup coffee for the same reason someone would do a wine tasting, try an array of cheeses, order a flight of beers... because it's educational, tasty, and, most importantly, fun.

There are three types of sensory information to consider when cupping:

Dry Fragrance – the smell of dry ground coffee

Aroma – the smell of the grounds combined with hot water

Flavor – the combination of the taste of liquid coffee and the aroma

In a professional setting, one silently makes note of how this sensory information changes over time. Silence is emphasized to avoid coloring someone else's individual impression with one's own ideas. Human perceptions are very suggestible, and often the mere mention of a flavor will leave it at the tip of one's tongue, waiting to be stamped onto any flavor that can't be readily identified. This is why it's best to share one's thoughts after the cupping is over. It is very important to share your thoughts, though, because this is how we see how well we're calibrated with one another. It also gives those less experienced cuppers a chance to learn.

MATERIALS

In addition to coffee, this is what you'll need to set up a cupping.

Bowls – There are bowls made specifically for this purpose (cupping bowls), but any 6- to 10-ounce bowl will do. My "cupping bowls" were $0.45 each at the Christmas Tree Shop.

Kettles – There are purpose-made pouring kettles that can be pretty affordable, but with care, a regular kettle, automatic water boiler, or even a saucepan will work, just as long as you have a water boiling and pouring system.

Spoons – There are purpose-made "cupping spoons," which are essentially deep soup spoons that facilitate quick movement and optimal volume. Cupping coffee with a cupping spoon is definitely the best way to do it, but a soup spoon will work fine as well. A regular spoon will also work in a pinch, though a fork will not. You will need at least two spoons.

Stopwatch – A timekeeper, like the one built into your phone, helps you keep track of brewing times and taste changes after the initial brew.

Scale – A simple scale with 0.1g accuracy is fine; no bluetooth-app-driven, overkill scale necessary. A quick search of the internet should yield many sub-$15 options. My favorite is the quick and responsive Palmscale 7.0, which is $35, but you've got to be a little careful as it's not waterproof.

Grinder – If you don't have a coffee grinder and you've made it this far in the book by choice, you deserve a coffee grinder! There are a bunch of hand grinders that are very affordable; I'm fond of my Hario hand grinder. There are also many electric grinders that are relatively affordable as well, but you do pay for the convenience of not having to turn the crank

yourself. There's a huge range, where you can quickly spend a lot on a very high quality grinder, but for this purpose, it isn't necessary to go overboard. Just make sure you go with a burr grinder, which will grind your coffee into more or less equal pieces, rather than a blade grinder, which will shred your coffee into wildly different shapes that will extract unevenly.

You'll also need another cup or two filled with rinse water for rinsing your spoons between cups. The size of these cups isn't important as long as your spoons fit. And that's it!

RECIPE

There are a range of different bowls or cups that are appropriate for cup tasting. Depending on the volume of your bowls, you'll use a different brewing recipe, unique to you. Now is the time to write that recipe.

Let's start by talking about brewing ratio, or the amount of coffee vs. the amount of water used in your brewing recipe. A good standard brewing ratio for cupping is one part coffee to seventeen parts water, 1:17. This leaves us with a cup that's not especially strong, which lets flavors come through without being muddled. You might prefer your coffee a little stronger, but it's important to taste clearly. That said, feel free to experiment and use your preferred ratio if you've got one.

In order to write our cupping recipe, we need to determine exactly how much water can fit into our bowls. You can do this by filling a bowl up with water on your gram scale and recording that number. To avoid overflowing our bowls when we have both water and coffee in the bowls, we'll dial that number back by 20 grams. This is the water portion of our recipe. Now, we can determine our dose of coffee with some quick math. To determine the dose, just divide the total water by 17.

Here's the process using my own cupping bowls. Filled to the brim, my cupping bowls fit exactly 160 grams of water. 160 minus 20 equals 140, so the water portion of my ratio is 140 grams. 140 divided by 17 is 8.2 (rounding to the nearest 0.1g). So that means my cupping recipe is 8.2 grams of coffee to 140 grams of water. Easy, right?

PROCESS

Set up one or two cups filled with rinse water so you can clean your spoon in between samples to avoid cross-contaminating flavors. While this hasn't historically been the norm, in the interest of hygiene, you should set up a separate cupping for everyone participating.

Set up – Assemble your materials. Get your water heating up. Weigh out your doses of coffee. I always set up at least two grams more than I'm actually going to put into my cupping bowl. One gram is for purging the grinder chute of the last coffee that was in there, the other gram is probably going to be retained by my grinder to some degree. Keep each dose in its respective bowl.

Grind – Before you grind your full dose for each cup, grind and dump one gram of that coffee to purge the remains of the last coffee that was in the grinder. (You can probably skip this part if you're using a hand grinder.) Next, grind your dose, and put the grounds in your bowl, verifying the weight using your scale. Repeat this

Smell – Smell the dry doses. This is like a teaser of what's to come. You'll know it if the coffee is about to be super fruity or funky.

Pour – Fill each bowl with filtered water, right off the boil, verifying the weight using your scale. Because different coffees will expand more or less depending on their age and roast level, the volume in the cupping bowl will end up being meaningfully different than the weight. For this reason, it is not accurate enough to eyeball the water. Complete this step shortly after grinding to help prevent the escape of aromatics.

Time – Start a stopwatch when you begin pouring. Smell the aroma. This is the start of the show; the aroma is going to continue to evolve over the next half hour or so, so be sure to keep smelling, and make notes.

Break – When the stopwatch reads four minutes, use your spoon to break the crust that has formed on each bowl. Do this by performing three gentle front to back stirs, dipping the spoon in about halfway. The purpose of this is to get all the coffee at the top to sink to the bottom, not to stir the whole thing. The act of breaking will release a flurry of aroma. Get a good whiff.

Clean – After breaking, use two spoons to clean stray grounds from the top of each bowl. With practice, you should be able to accomplish this in one smooth motion, using both spoons to trace the perimeter and cover the whole surface of the bowl. It's important that you keep the spoons up at the surface and don't agitate the grounds down at the bottom of the bowl.

Wait – Wait until the stopwatch reads ten minutes.

Clean again – After a few minutes of sitting, oils will begin to form on the surface. These oils will coat your tongue and interfere with tasting. Use your two spoons to scoop the oil slick off as well.

Taste – After the second cleaning, you're good to start tasting.

Take a spoonful of the coffee, and give it a good slurp. Think about what you're tasting. Make notes. At first, write down whatever comes into your head, stream-of-consciousness. If you're using a cupping form (more on this shortly), start to fill it out. Take a taste of each coffee on the table, making sure to rinse your spoon between cups. Think about the differences between the cups. What makes each of these coffees uniquely that coffee? Which coffees are the most different? Taste those side by side. Your impressions will begin to take more concrete shape as you come to terms with the differences.

Take a pause, then repeat this process. Keep making notes and filling out your form as the full picture of each coffee starts to take shape. You'll notice big changes as the coffees cool. Some coffees will start out somewhat uninspiring, then really open up into their full glory as perceived acidity increases. Some coffees will start out wild and unique, then cool into unpleasant and boozy. As you start to build a better picture of the coffee, try and rein in the language in your notes. What are you really tasting? How do each of the coffees compare to each other in regard to the basic tastes? Which is sweetest? Which is the brightest? Are the flavors balanced, or is one shouting louder than the others? Think about the aromatic compounds you've learned. Are any of those nice sounding aroma descriptions ringing true? How about the not so nice aromas?

People familiar with tasting wine or spirits will know that swirling wine in its glass will release lots of aromatics, and the same applies to coffee. While swirling cupping bowls isn't possible, you can still get swirly while cupping. Scoop a few spoonfuls into another vessel like a brandy snifter, then swirl and evaluate the aroma in that vessel. I prefer doing this to bending all the way down and shoving my nose up to the surface of the cupping bowl, as standing up straight allows you to take full, easy breaths. This method also ensures that the aromatics of the coffee you're evaluating are isolated from the other coffees on the table.

But why do I have to slurp?

Slurping serves a few purposes. The most important reason is because it sprays coffee over all of your palate, so you can utilize all those eager little taste buds. It also cools the coffee, but, if you wait ten minutes to start tasting like I suggest, it won't be scalding when you dive in anyway. Finally, slurping is fun! You don't have to, but I really encourage you to ignore how stupid you feel slurping loudly and just get into the funny noises you can make. With practice, it's possible to make a loud laser beam noise as you slurp, which is obviously the goal. Just make sure you're slurping into your mouth, not directly into your lungs (as even a seasoned coffee taster can be prone to do), which will cause you to cough and splutter, much to your embarrassment.

BLIND CUPPING

Confirmation bias is huge for humans. We expect things to be a certain way, and we have a tendency to quickly draw conclusions based on our expectations, failing to take in new information. For example, an experienced taster may think that they know what Brazilian coffees taste like, so if they taste a cup that's labeled "Brazil" they'll say, "Ah yes, Brazilian coffee. Good thing I'm so experienced. I know that Brazilian coffees are nutty and chocolatey, so I barely have to focus right now." They'll identify nutty and chocolatey flavors and move on, potentially missing something special. But, given the same coffee with an unlabeled cup, they might fail to identify the origin and have to really challenge themselves to taste critically, not relying on generalizations, to paint a mental picture of what makes this particular coffee unique. This is why blind cupping is of paramount importance.

As you set up each bowl, start by putting a label on the bottom, where you can't see it. If there's at least two of you tasting, have one person do the labeling and the other person mix them up on the table. If you're going solo, it's usually enough to set a few tiers where you can completely lose track of which is which. When I'm cupping by myself, I label each bowl with unground beans, keeping them in a jumble on the table, so I don't let them get into any order. Then, I'll grind them, continuing not to organize the bowls. Finally, I'll mix them up a good amount before I line them up and pour the water.

Some of the tasting challenges coming up are a little harder to set up as a blind tasting by yourself because they involve either different waters or they have some sort of manipulation of the cup after the water is poured. I would encourage you to pick up an inexpensive lazy Susan or some sort of turntable-type-thing, if you don't have one already, and let that help you in mixing up these cups if you're going solo.

DEFECTS

One of the most important aspects of cupping coffee is recognizing and identifying defects present in the cup. Defects can be inherent in the green coffee due to damage before harvest (through environmental factors like soil, weather, other crops stealing resources, or pests), poor processing, or damage during storage or shipment. They can also be produced through poor handling in the roaster.

An extremely educational but equally unpleasant exercise is cupping a spread of defect coffee. While it is good to put names to defects, like the infamous dishwatery "Rio Flavor," I wouldn't recommend it for someone not working in the industry. That said, recognizing defective products is a right every consumer should have.

Some flavors to look for that say "green coffee defect" are pronounced woody or cereal flavors, chemical or medicinal flavors, strong unpleasant fermentedness, must, mold, vinegar, foul rotten fish, or dishwater. Some roast specific defects include savory or grassy flavors, sour underripe flavors, paper, and carbon or charcoal. Yum. The presence of any of these flavors means there's a problem.

Some of these defects result from individual beans that are easy to spot visually, so an attentive barista might be able to catch them before serving if it comes to that. If you've ever seen a competition level barista spread out and sort their coffee beans, this is why. A single pronounced defect in the cup will result in poor scores at the competition level, so sorting is imperative.

The home barista or coffee enthusiast can benefit from sorting as well if they have the time for it. All you have to do is spread the coffee out and remove any beans that look very different from the rest. Broken bits or empty husks, oddly colored beans, unevenly roasted beans, shriveled beans, etc. are all something you can remove and expect an improvement in cup quality. Additionally, if you notice the coffee you're buying frequently contains a lot of irregular beans, it could be an indicator of poor quality control at the roaster, so that's something to consider.

Here are a few specific defects you can easily identify after the

roast:

Beans damaged by an insect called the coffee berry borer will appear pockmarked and full of holes or tunnels, very dark after roasting in comparison to other beans, and will taste bitter and tarry in the cup.

Quakers are beans from immature or underripe cherries. You can spot them easily because they still look green after the roast. They contribute bitter, green, chemical, or fermentedness to the cup. Watch out, though: beans with this appearance might also be caused by roasted coffee being passed through the same bins or chutes as green coffee and picking up the stragglers.

Black beans result from poor practices prior to or during processing and are more common with natural processed coffee. They look dull and yellow after roasting, and result in pronounced off flavors.

There are also a few common "defects" that appear in the cup that are not really the fault of the coffee but are more like "user error." Dirty brewing equipment can certainly put an off flavor in the cup. Another one that might arise ironically fixing the first is the dish soap tasting "defect" that comes from dish soap not being rinsed adequately. Water temperature and chemistry can have a huge impact in the cup as well; a kettle filled with tap water instead of filtered water can lead to surprising off flavors, especially if you're used to the filtered stuff. These are just a few examples of why you might want to turn the lens on yourself when trying to solve flavor issues.

5. Adding Form to the Process

A cupping form is a very helpful thing to have during the process of tasting, as it provides an organized method for evaluation of all the aspects of a coffee you consider to be worth noting. While you're cupping, it can be very easy to fixate on one flavor and spend all your mental energy trying to place it or focus all your attention on one aspect of the coffees, like the acidity. A lack of structure will result in a directionless and overall unproductive session, and structure is what cupping forms are all about.

A cupping form lays out all the different aspects of the flavor of a coffee, leaving us little opportunity to miss something. Sometimes this checklist-like approach to breaking down a coffee can bring us big insights into its traits that we would have missed if we were in another frame of mind.

In a professional setting, a cupping form with a point system is used to score coffees. As various organizations have different standards for calibration when it comes to tasting and use different scoring systems, scoring coffee is more of an internal means for one organization to talk about coffee quality amongst themselves. Having a team that is very well calibrated with one another means that problems can be quickly isolated because everyone knows what constitutes a problem. Individual baristas can write recipes on their own, using their team's calibration standards as a guide, and consumers can come to expect reliability and consistency in flavor quality. The way calibration is established is by making sure every team member is using the same vocabulary and is on the same page when it comes to scoring.

Outside of a professional environment, scoring carries a good deal less weight; but that's not to say it has no place anywhere else. If an individual keeps track of all the coffees they taste and looks back on their previous tastings thoughtfully, they might develop for themselves a scoring system that makes sense and will give them a mental framework to quickly evaluate coffees.

The key point here is that this type of personal development takes time. The professional or the home barista should be aware that for those first few tasting sessions, scores aren't going to mean much, because they don't yet have a frame of reference built up. But over time, they will be able to notice when a coffee has remarkable characteristics in a given category and score it accordingly.

I think one of the most valuable experiences you can have while scoring coffees outside of a professional setting is comparing your scores with those of an established organization. This type of comparison is possible when tasting a Cup of Excellence coffee, or other such coffee where you can look up the scores online, or by asking the roaster where you got the coffee if you might be able to take a look at their cupping scores. This type of comparison is valuable because it gives you an immediate frame of reference for these abstract numbers, which can seem meaningless at the start.

I think the best way to start cup tasting with forms is to taste two coffees comparatively, using a very simple form to rank which is higher in a few easy categories. Next, move on to tasting multiple coffees, using a sliding scale without numbers to rank the categories. It will be easy to assign values along the sliding scale comparatively, and you won't be burdened

by the conundrum of assigning a score of 7 when you don't yet know what a score of 7 should really mean. Then, when you've got a lot of coffees under your belt, you'll have a much more robust frame of reference if you choose to add scoring or move to an established professional cupping form.

You can find free printable PDF versions of all three of these upcoming cupping forms on my website at the url:

barrytaft.com/forms

I recommend printing them out and writing all over them.

HEAD TO HEAD FORM

your name:

Coffee A__________

balanced? yes no

notes:

Coffee B__________

balanced? yes no

notes:

aroma

sweet

acid

bitter

body

finish

This form is very simple to use. Does the coffee have a balanced flavor? Indicate yes or no. Indicate on the appropriate line which coffee is more intense in each of the six categories. If you think there's a tie, put a mark in the middle of the line.

If one coffee is considerably more intense in a category, put a mark all the way on that coffee's end. Mark somewhere in between if the intensities in a category are closer together.

Make sure to note your thoughts on each of the categories in the notes section and keep in mind the lines are indicating intensity, not perceived pleasantness; a coffee with a higher intensity in a given category doesn't "win."

The categories are:

Aroma – Which coffee smells stronger? It can be easier to discern aroma by transferring a couple spoonfuls of coffee into a vessel like a brandy snifter or Glencairn glass and evaluating there, just be sure to rinse between samples.

Sweet – Which coffee is sweeter? Keep in mind sweetness in coffee is much more subtle than soda or candy. Sometimes it will be more apparent as a lingering sweetness after you swallow.

Acid – Which coffee has a more pronounced acidity? Try separating the basic tastes from the aromatics by plugging your nose with coffee in your mouth. It should then be easier to separate sweet, acid, and bitter.

Bitter – Which has a higher bitterness?

Body – Which coffee has a richer body? Think water vs milk or broth.

Finish – Which coffee has a longer or more distinct finish after

you've swallowed?

SLIDING SCALE FORM

your name:

Coffee A

sweet ____ acid ____ bitter ____

aroma ____ body ____ finish ____

notes:

Coffee B

sweet ____ acid ____ bitter ____

aroma ____ body ____ finish ____

notes:

Coffee C

sweet ____ acid ____ bitter ____

aroma ____ body ____ finish ____

notes:

Coffee D

sweet ____ acid ____ bitter ____

aroma ____ body ____ finish ____

notes:

Coffee E

sweet ____ acid ____ bitter ____

aroma ____ body ____ finish ____

notes:

This form has all the same categories as the head to head form, except it has space for five different coffees. The goal with this form is to taste all the coffees comparatively and indicate where the coffees stand in the different categories. A mark all the way at the left of the line represents the lowest intensity, and a mark all the way at the right represents the highest intensity. It takes a little more nuance figuring out where to mark along the lines when comparing more than two coffees. That said, it should still be pretty straightforward as long as you are tasting thoughtfully. Make the round of the table thinking about one category at a time. Bringing order to the coffees in the middle is where the challenge lies.

Something I like to do whenever I'm done tasting for the day after cupping multiple coffees is go with my gut and pick a winner. Which coffee stood up the best over time? Regularly choosing your personal favorite will help you to quickly identify these table winning characteristics in other coffees.

SCORING FORM

name:
date:

Coffee A

aroma(dry) -2 -1 0 1 2	clean -2 -1 0 1 2	sweet -2 -1 0 1 2	acid -2 -1 0 1 2	balance -2 -1 0 1 2
aroma(wet) -2 -1 0 1 2	flavor -2 -1 0 1 2	body -2 -1 0 1 2	finish -2 -1 0 1 2	overall -2 -1 0 1 2

notes:

total points + 80 = ☐

Coffee B

aroma(dry) -2 -1 0 1 2	clean -2 -1 0 1 2	sweet -2 -1 0 1 2	acid -2 -1 0 1 2	balance -2 -1 0 1 2
aroma(wet) -2 -1 0 1 2	flavor -2 -1 0 1 2	body -2 -1 0 1 2	finish -2 -1 0 1 2	overall -2 -1 0 1 2

notes:

total points + 80 = ☐

Coffee C

aroma(dry) -2 -1 0 1 2	clean -2 -1 0 1 2	sweet -2 -1 0 1 2	acid -2 -1 0 1 2	balance -2 -1 0 1 2
aroma(wet) -2 -1 0 1 2	flavor -2 -1 0 1 2	body -2 -1 0 1 2	finish -2 -1 0 1 2	overall -2 -1 0 1 2

notes:

total points + 80 = ☐

Coffee D

aroma(dry) -2 -1 0 1 2	clean -2 -1 0 1 2	sweet -2 -1 0 1 2	acid -2 -1 0 1 2	balance -2 -1 0 1 2
aroma(wet) -2 -1 0 1 2	flavor -2 -1 0 1 2	body -2 -1 0 1 2	finish -2 -1 0 1 2	overall -2 -1 0 1 2

notes:

total points + 80 = ☐

Coffee E

aroma(dry) -2 -1 0 1 2	clean -2 -1 0 1 2	sweet -2 -1 0 1 2	acid -2 -1 0 1 2	balance -2 -1 0 1 2
aroma(wet) -2 -1 0 1 2	flavor -2 -1 0 1 2	body -2 -1 0 1 2	finish -2 -1 0 1 2	overall -2 -1 0 1 2

notes:

total points + 80 = ☐

This form adds a few categories the other forms don't have, as well as a scoring system. All coffees come in with a base score of 80, and they can earn or lose points throughout the cupping to come up with a final score. With the points system, we're moving away from the intensity scales of the last forms and transitioning to a score based on the quality of each category. For instance, a coffee with a sharp, biting acidity should not score high even though it is intense, because that attribute is not pleasing to the palate. Think about the numbers like this: zeros across the board leaves us with a grade of B, which is a perfectly drinkable, okay cup of coffee. One should only add or remove points in the case of exceptionally good or bad qualities. (More on defects later.)

Remember to take as many notes as you can. The new categories with this form are:

Aroma (dry) – This is the dry fragrance of the ground coffee.

Aroma (wet) – This is the aroma of the coffee and hot water. Make sure to evaluate this when you first pour the water, as well as throughout the cupping.

Clean (or "clean cup") – Any sort of earthiness, mustiness, or general "offness" that masks the pleasant flavors loses the coffee points in clean cup. A coffee scoring high in this category has a remarkable clarity.

Balance – Instead of a yes/no item, here we're giving balance a score. A high score in this category means that every aspect of this coffee is singing in perfect harmony.

Flavor – This is an overarching category covering the overall

impression of the flavor (aroma+basic tastes).

Overall – This is a catch-all category covering the overall impression of all aspects of the coffee.

OTHER FORMS

The scoring system I present in this book favors simplicity and ease of general application over specific use cases and exhaustive rigor when it comes to scores. As I mentioned earlier, many organizations have their own cupping forms and protocols, and it can be enormously educational to see how different reputable organizations approach the process as it applies to their needs. A few I'd recommend taking a look at are the Cup of Excellence form, which is designed to evaluate coffees all hailing from the same country of origin, the Specialty Coffee Association form, and the Analytic Cupping Scorecard from Cafe Imports, all of which can be found with a quick Google search and are thoroughly different from each other.

In addition to these forms, your favorite roasters almost certainly have cupping forms and protocols which they follow, even your favorite coffee bar might as well, and you shouldn't be hesitant to ask about them. Many professionals in the industry will relish an opportunity to talk about the lengths they go to in order to ensure high quality, as these steps usually go completely unnoticed. I wouldn't be surprised if they'd bewilling to share their cupping form with an eager guest. This is also a great way to get the inside scoop on which coffees are performing best amongst staff.

6. Challenging Your Sensory Skills

This final chapter is dedicated to challenges that will help you improve your coffee tasting skills. Much like the "sensory siblings" section, these challenges are structured and informative, but I also find them to be quite entertaining and fun.

Most of these challenges are based around triangulations. Triangulations are a tasting exercise where we take three samples: two are identical, and one is an odd one out. The goal of the exercise is to correctly choose the odd one out. The beauty of triangulations is that they range from super easy to ludicrously difficult, and everywhere in between. Both the most infant-like novice and the most machine-like super-taster will be able to create triangulations that challenge them and help them improve.

I'm breaking these challenges up into two categories: exercises where you try and separate different coffees, and exercises where you try to separate different preparations of the same coffee.

Separating different coffees is a great way to learn about origins and processing, and will be fun for an enthusiast, even if they fail at the exercises.

Separating different preparations of the same coffee is more like solving a puzzle, and they're a great way to learn about the effect of brewing parameters on flavor.

I'm also breaking these challenges into difficulty categories. All of them will start with the simplest version of the exercise, a basic triangulation. The basic triangulation will be followed by two different degrees of difficulty. You should be able to quickly ascertain which difficulty level is appropriate for you. A beginner working through the simple triangulations will realize which challenges are easy for them, and which ones will need a little work. If none of these exercises are difficult for you, then damn, you're a pro.

In order to ensure your best performance, it's advisable to avoid especially flavorful or spicy foods leading up to tasting, as well as smoking and booze. It also helps to prime your palate with a little coffee to give yourself a baseline, so don't think you need to skip your morning coffee. Finally, having a palate refresher around like unflavored crackers or unflavored sparkling water will definitely help if you're experiencing palate fatigue mid-tasting.

There are certainly tricks to solving these triangulations, but I don't think you'll improve your tasting skills if I give them away, though I'll certainly explain what's going on. I think it's important that you perform these exercises, tasting critically, and find out the solution yourself. Make sure you're using your notebook or cupping form, as there is much less impact if you aren't writing things down to look back on later. The key to retaining knowledge and improving is reflection. Make sure you're asking yourself questions. What are my takeaways here? What could I have done differently to improve my performance? Why am I doing this to myself?

MULTIPLE COFFEE EXERCISES

Tastings between two different coffees are fun and can be quite challenging. They are also a fantastic way of learning about coffee origins, processing, and your own personal preferences.

If buying several different bags of coffee at once is not financially doable, you could round up some friends and go in as a group on several coffees at once. That way everyone comes away with their own bag of coffee at the end but gets to taste them all. This also sets the stage for tasting as a group, which is ideal.

Your local roaster or coffee house might be willing to help out here as well. When you go in to buy a bag, tell them about what you're doing, and ask if they might be willing to part ways with a few small doses of different coffees in addition to your purchase. You only really need a small amount of each coffee, which is not an unreasonable request given you've already made a purchase. Even if you're not asking for doses, meeting an enthusiastic, engaged guest like this can be the highlight of a barista's day, and many will be eager to talk and look forward to hearing about your progress.

A couple notes before we dive in: First, while I believe everyone is entitled to their personal preference on roast degree, when trying to differentiate two different single origins, a dark roast will mask the defining characteristics of the coffees. If you're seriously trying to learn about coffee flavor, you should choose coffees with a less heavy-handed roast. Second, except where noted, I would recommend sticking with washed process coffees, at least until you start to get more advanced at tasting.

Coffees from Different Places

This exercise is very simple, we're just separating coffees from different places, but it has a lot of depth. There are literally endless variations, it's a lot of fun, and it's enormously educational. I would encourage revisiting it often. If you're ever in a situation where you're at a blind cupping that is not of your creation, add a layer of challenge for yourself by performing a variation of this exercise on your notepad.

A Simple Triangulation:

Let's start by separating the continents. One of the easiest exercises would be differentiating a Kenyan coffee from a Brazilian coffee, but that's just an example; there are many options here. Once you get the feel for this exercise, ditch the triangulation approach and set up a blind cupping with a flight of coffees. The challenge is to move the African coffees to one side of the table, and the coffees from the Americas to the other, or identifying and separating African, American, and Asian coffees. (You get the idea.)

Add Some Difficulty:

Once you're comfortable separating the continents, try breaking it down to individual countries within the continents. Can you separate Kenyan coffee from Ethiopian coffee? Can you separate Guatemalan coffee from Colombian coffee? Later, you can try and separate different growing regions within one country, then move on to different farms within one growing region.

A Serious Challenge:

Set up a blind cupping with as many coffees as you want. It's best if you don't know what's on the table beforehand. Match each coffee with its country of origin, only revealing a list of the countries when you're stumped. Can you call out variety, processing, specific growing region, or even the farm or specific coffees you're tasting?

Different Processing

Processing method has an enormous impact in the cup. Washed coffees will tend to taste the most "clean"; naturals and honey processes will introduce different degrees of fruit and funk into the cup. Naturals can be very polarizing, and there's definitely a spectrum of clean tasting naturals to very boozy-funky-barnyard naturals.

A Simple Triangulation:

Try and differentiate a washed and a natural processed coffee from the same country (ideally the same farm). Or try and differentiate a washed and semi-washed or honey process, or a natural and a honey process.

Add Some Difficulty:

Set up a flight of coffees for a blind cupping with several washed coffees as well as several naturals. Separate them into their respective categories.

A Serious Challenge:

Same as above, but let's include lots of processes. Here's some ideas: Can you differentiate between different degrees of honey processing (white, red, black, etc.)? Can you differentiate between naturals and carbonic maceration, or anaerobic fermentation coffees? Without a list of the processes on the table, could you call out the processing for each coffee? If you were given a table full of naturals with multiple cups each, could you separate them?

Different Varieties

An invaluable experience that I wish was more frequently available is tasting different coffee varieties grown on the same farm side by side. It's very interesting considering the differences and similarities between the coffees. Assuming the same processing, the differences should all be down to the variety, which will give you a very nice picture of what makes each of these varieties unique.

It is incredibly valuable getting to know a variety well. Wine is all about variety, and most entry level wine drinkers know a sauvignon blanc from a chardonnay, but coffee hasn't gotten there to the same degree. I think this is an area the industry could use a boost wherever it interfaces with consumers.

On the flip side, any similarities you find between these coffees can be attributed to terroir, which is a rather nice deep dive into the impact of soil and growing conditions on the farm. If you see this type of offering available from any roaster, I recommend grabbing it.

A Simple Triangulation:

Can you triangulate different varieties grown on the same farm?

Add Some Difficulty:

Can you identify which is which in the triangulation above?

A Serious Challenge:

Could you arrange and identify a table of different varieties? If you had three different Bourbons and three different Typicas, could you separate them? Could you separate pacas, maragogype, and pacamara?

Same Variety, Different Farm

This exercise is similar to the Coffees from Different Places exercise, but we're removing a variable. Assuming the same processing method, the differences you find between the cups in this exercise should be down to the terroir of the different farms, and the similarities should be down to the variety. Of course, this is true on paper, but in reality, harvest, milling, hulling, and sorting are carried out differently at different farms, and the impact these processes can have on the cup can't be dismissed. The handling of green coffee after it leaves the farm can have a big impact on flavor as well, the conditions during shipping, for instance. In a perfect world, you would perform this exercise with coffees grown by one producer on a large farm, where there could be meaningful differences of terroir between two patches, but they would still be guaranteed the same treatment after harvest. That said, this exercise is the only meaningful way to really try and grasp the impact of terroir on flavor in the cup.

A Simple Triangulation:

Could you identify the odd one out in a triangulation of the same variety grown at different farms?

Add Some Difficulty:

Same as above, but the farms are in the same growing region.

A Serious Challenge:

Could you separate a table of the same variety into their countries of origin? How about their growing regions or farms?

One Coffee, Different Roast Profile

Small changes in the roasting process can have a massive impact on the flavors present in the cup. This is a great way to come to grips with exactly what is changing in the cup as we bring coffee further into development. It's easy during this exercise to leap immediately on the obvious changes, but equally important to note are how the coffees retain their character, what's the same between the two.

Those working at a coffee roastery can undertake this experiment to a greater degree by pulling out samples at several stages during the roasting of one batch. If you're chummy with a coffee roaster, they might be willing to let you follow a coffee on its journey from underdeveloped to fully developed. For those without an in at the coffee roaster, many roasters offer espresso and filter roasts of the same coffee, the exercise below is geared towards those offerings.

A Simple Triangulation:

Set up a triangulation to see if you can tell the difference between filter and espresso roast of the same single origin. See if you can accomplish the triangulation by smell alone before tasting.

Add Some Difficulty:

Make two blends by weighing and blending the two different roast profiles, one that's 30% filter, 70% espresso, and one that's 70% filter, 30% espresso, can you triangulate those?

A Serious Challenge:

How about a 60%/40%? Could you arrange a table where the ratio is different in every cup?

One Coffee, Different Age

Here we are trying to tell the difference between two roasts of the same coffee, the difference being one was roasted some time ago, and one was roasted recently. In a perfect world, we would have a time machine that we could age coffee with so we could use the same roast batch for both cups. Sadly this is not in the cards as of this writing. This experiment will go best if you can verify with the roaster that it is in fact the same coffee being roasted, not two different Colombian coffees being released under one name, for instance. Some roasters might have old coffee which is beyond their shelf-life standards available at the same time you buy your fresh coffee, but it's also easy to save a dose or two for this challenge.

A Simple Triangulation:

For the easy one, try a difference of around a month, making sure one of these coffees is as fresh as possible.

Add Some Difficulty:

Bring it down to two weeks difference, try 7 days off roast and 21 days off roast.

A Serious Challenge: Bring it closer together still.

Same Coffee, Different Roaster

Many roasters work with the same importing companies or go in together on coffee to offset the cost. Because of this it's quite easy to find two different roaster's versions of the same coffee. This is another interesting way to see the effects of roasting style on the final cup.

A Simple Triangulation:

Could you separate them in a triangulation?

Add Some Difficulty:

Can you identify which is which? What's the difference?

A Serious Challenge:

Can you differentiate between different ratio blends of the two roasts (as in the different roast profiles challenge)?

Blending

Blending coffee well is challenging. For one thing, some coffees sing a lot louder than others and will mask more delicate coffees completely. Many coffees will also have different solubilities, so it might never be possible to get all components of a blend perfectly dialed-in in one brewing recipe. Fortunately for us, because of the challenges that blends present, they make devilishly tricky tasting exercises.

A Simple Triangulation:

Can you differentiate between two coffees, one of which is

a single origin, the other is a 50/50 blend by weight of that coffee and another single origin? Start by blending two coffees that were easy to distinguish in the Coffees from Different Places challenge, then move on to coffees with a more similar flavor profile.

Add Some Difficulty:

There's room for a huge number of variations in this challenge. To add some difficulty, This time all the cups are blends, start with 70/30 vs. 30/70. Try and work in a third coffee to one or all of the blends.

A Serious Challenge:

This is a fun one. Make a flight of different single origins, along with one cup that is a blend of some, but not all of those single origins. Can you pick out the blend components? I'd start with a two part blend, then move up to three or more.

Could you identify the blend components of two different blends? Could you pick out a blend containing a component that wasn't included in the flight?

ONE-COFFEE EXERCISES

These exercises are more budget friendly, but I think they are more like puzzles to solve and can be quite tricky. It can be maddening trying to distinguish very, very small changes to brewing parameters. While some of the exercises in the previous section could still provide a nice learning experience if not performed blind, these one-coffee exercises will be destroyed by confirmation bias and provide no value at all if you know which cup has the changes. In addition to simply being a great way to sharpen your palate, I think these exercises make a fantastic introduction to the difference changing brewing parameters makes.

A one-coffee tasting exercise which I'm not including is picking out different brew methods, like V60 vs Aeropress. Aside from being outside the cupping format of all the other exercises, I'm not including this exercise because changing the brewing method is really changing multiple brewing parameters at once, and for this reason is not as educational as the other exercises. What I mean by this is: when we take a Chemex brewer vs. a Hario V60 brewer, we're not simply changing the filter paper (which affects body). A thicker filter paper will also increase the brew time affecting extraction, we're also changing the brewing coffee bed geometry, the heat retention and thermal stability of the brewing device (glass vs. plastic, ceramic, or metal), pouring technique also changes because of the differences in distance from the top of the brewer to the coffee bed... you get the idea.

Changing Up the Dose

Changing dose affects the brew ratio. In a cupping, this impacts the concentration. In a filter coffee or espresso, changing the dose will also impact extraction. For example, lowering the dose in an espresso will increase extraction, if we leave our final beverage weight unchanged, because less water will be absorbed, resulting in more water passing through the grounds.

A Simple Triangulation:

Three cups of the same coffee, one of them is made with a dose of 1.5 grams more than the other.

Add Some Difficulty:

Can you separate coffees with a 0.5g difference?

A Serious Challenge:

How about 0.2? Could you put a table full of bowls in the correct order from lowest to highest dose?

Changing Up the Grind Size

Changing the grind size will impact extraction, as finer particle sizes offer more surface area for water to interact with. Generally speaking, coffees that are underextracted taste sour and coffees that are overextracted taste bitter.

A Simple Triangulation:

Try and solve a triangulation where you're picking between coffees ground at a different setting. Not too far apart, but not literally the next setting over either.

Add Some Difficulty:

This might start out easy, but it will get harder as you bring the settings closer together.

A Serious Challenge:

Try and arrange a table where all the cups are ground at different settings.

Different Water Chemistry

You might be surprised by the difference the brewing water chemistry makes in cup quality. Generally speaking, softer waters bring out acidity, while harder water mutes acidity. Different mineral makeup will impact extraction in different ways, with magnesium ions extracting more citric and malic acids than calcium ions.[32]

A Simple Triangulation:

Can you solve a triangulation where you're differentiating cups made with filtered water vs. tap water? It's important you verify the water is the same temperature before pouring.

Add Some Difficulty:

Can you do this with filtered water and another type of filtered water? You could try different brands of filter jugs, different bottled waters, or even filtered water vs. distilled water mixed with Third Wave Water or your own remineralization solution?

A Serious Challenge:

If you were given a spread of coffees, all brewed with filtered water remineralized to different degrees, could you sort them based on water hardness? Could you organize a table where the element changing is the amount of the buffer? How about organizing a spread with one filtered water brew, one filtered water plus extra magnesium brew, and one filtered water plus extra calcium carbonate brew? How about five cups where we add the minerals in different degrees?

Different Water Temperature

Water temperature impacts extraction, with hotter water increasing overall extraction. As you'll remember from the aroma section, some aromatic compounds need very hot water to be extracted at all. What else do you think is changing?

A Simple Triangulation:

Can you solve a triangulation where the factor we're changing is water temperature? Start with water right off the boil (210F) vs. water at 170F. Can you solve the triangulation with your nose alone?

Add Some Difficulty:

Bring the lower temperature up. Try 180 vs. 210, 190 vs. 210, and 200 vs. 210. Is there a point where this gets really difficult?

A Serious Challenge:

Could you arrange a table where all the cups were brewed at different temperatures?

Stirring

Stirring, or agitation, increases extraction.

A Simple Triangulation:

This is a triangulation where we pick out stirred vs. unstirred coffee. When it's time to break, give one or two of the cups a stir all the way to the bottom. Make sure you stir the exact same way each time. Start with five stirs front to back, dialing back the stirring if that's too easy.

Add Some Difficulty:

Give them all a stir, try and pick out the difference between different amounts of stirring. Five stirs vs. one stir for instance.

A Serious Challenge:

Try and organize a table where each cup has a different amount of stirring.

Filtering

Different filtering methods will alter the body and clarity of the resulting brew to different degrees. Generally speaking, metal mesh filters will let through many more solids and oils than paper filters, and thus metal mesh filtered coffee will be fuller bodied and have less clarity, and paper filters will result in lighter body and more clarity.

A Simple Triangulation:

All the brewing parameters are the same here, except after ten minutes, instead of beginning tasting, we're going to put the contents of each cup through a filter. Make sure to perform this transfer the same way for each cup. The challenge is to try and tell the difference between different filtering methods. Try French press vs. any paper filter. You'll be able to tell the difference visually, so avoid looking at what you're tasting.

Add Some Difficulty:

Try Cloth filter vs. paper filter.

A Serious Challenge:

Try different brands of paper filters.

Conclusion

Well, you've made it to the end. There's so much depth to tasting that I certainly couldn't comprehensively contain it within the confines of this book, nor am I qualified to do so. I do hope that this has been a solid introduction, or if you came in with a fair amount of knowledge, I hope you were able to get something new out of it!

If you're looking for more, I have some great book recommendations in the following section, but of course, reading will only get you so far. Keep tasting, tasting, tasting!

My favorite part of the discipline of tasting is that the more you learn, the more there inevitably is to be learned. Tastes change over time, for instance, in the specialty coffee scene the espresso shots we were pulling ten years ago taste very different from those that I pull when working the bar today.

Styles will absolutely continue to change.

Our palates also change over time, our skills become more refined, we narrow in on the tastes that we enjoy, and we learn why it is that we enjoy them. Then, as we age the number of taste buds we have starts to decrease, our perception of smells changes, and the tastes we enjoy continue to change as well. Everything is always changing, everything is ephemeral, and because of this we have to stay humble!

Acknowledgements

I'd like to thank some of my mentors, friends, and peers in this industry who I've learned from and bounced ideas off of over the years: Marley Brush, Liza Shirazi, Liz Cohen, Dan Demers, Sam Harake, Yoshinori Uda, Chris Marinuzzi, Meghann Louie-Heintell, Hana Vered, Tracy Jiang, Art Garcia, Kris Dewey, Kristina Jackson, Matthew Magnuson, and especially Ahmed Abdalla for his persistent encouragement on this project.

A big thanks to my editor Dan Crissman for his invaluable structural input and advice.

Further Reading

In addition to the references that follow, I can't overstate the value I've found in the following books during the creation of this one:

Coffee Flavor Chemistry, Ivon Flament

Coffee Growing, Processing, and Sustainable Production, Wintgens et al

The Coffee Roaster's Companion, Scott Rao

The Flavor Matrix, James Briscione

Flavor: The Science of Our Most Neglected Sense, Bob Holmes

Neurogastronomy, Gordon Shepherd

Philosophy of Olfactory Perception, Andreas Keller

References

1 Sarah Mae Sincero (Mar 18, 2013). Neural Pathways of Smell, Taste, and Touch. Retrieved Dec 06, 2021 from Explorable.com: https://explorable.com/neural-pathways-of-smell-taste-and-touch

2 "How does our sense of taste work?" InformedHealth, National Center for Biotechnology Information. December 20, 2011, https://www.ncbi.nlm.nih.gov/books/NBK279408/. Accessed December 18, 2019.

3 "Taste, olfactory, and food texture processing ..." National Center for Biotechnology Information. https://www.ncbi.nlm.nih.gov/pubmed/15924905. Accessed December 22, 2019.

4 Sabrina Stierwalt "Why Do Smells Trigger Memories?" Scientific American. https://www.scientificamerican.com/article/why-do-smells-trigger-memories1/ Accessed December 6, 2021

5 "Mammalian Sweet Taste Receptors," National Center for Biotechnology Information https://pubmed.ncbi.nlm.nih.gov/11509186. Accessed June 17,6 2020

6 Folmer, Britta. "The Craft and Science of Coffee."

7 University of Southern California. "Researchers hone in on the elusive receptor for sour taste." ScienceDaily. ScienceDaily, 19 September 2019. www.sciencedaily.com/releases/2019/09/190919142308.htm. Accessed June 17, 2020.

8 Rao, Scott. The Coffee Roaster's Companion

9 "T2Rs Function as Bitter Taste Receptors," Cell. https://

www.cell.com/abstract/S0092-8674(00)80706-0. Accessed 10 June 17, 2020.

10 Holmes, Bob. "Flavor: The Science of Our Most Neglected Sense".

11 "Coffee Chemistry and Coffee Aroma" CoffeeResearch.org. http://www.coffeeresearch.org/science/aromamain.htm. Accessed June 17, 2020.

12 Blank, I., Sen, A. & Grosch, W. Potent odorants of the roasted powder and brew of Arabica coffee. Z Lebensm Unters Forch 195, 239–245 (1992). https://doi.org/10.1007/BF01202802

13 "Subthreshold Olfactory Stimulation Can Enhance Sweetness," Chemical Senses, Volume 32, Issue 3, March 2007, Pages 205–214, https://academic.oup.com/chemse/article/32/3/205/371962. Accessed August 7, 2020.

14 Sanchez Lopez, Jose & Wellinger, Marco & Glöss, Alexia & Zimmermann, Ralf & Yeretzian, Chahan. (2016). Extraction Kinetics of Coffee Aroma Compounds using a Semi-Automatic Machine: On-Line Analysis by PTR-ToF-MS. International Journal of Mass Spectrometry. 401. 10.1016/j.ijms.2016.02.015.

15 Mestdagh, Frédéric et al. "The kinetics of coffee aroma extraction." Food Research International 63 (2014): 271-274.

16 "Coffee: Production, Quality and Chemistry CHAPTER 33. Coffee Volatile and Aroma Compounds" December 20, 2019, https://www.researchgate.net/ publication/330334396_CHAPTER_33_Coffee_Volatile_and_ Aroma_Compounds_-_From_the_Green_Bean_to_the_Cup_Pro- duction_Quality_and_Chemistry. Accessed June 18, 2020.

17 "Creating the future of coffee" World Coffee Research.

https://worldcoffeeresearch.org/media/documents/2018_Annual_Report.pdf. Accessed November 13, 2020.

18 Information such as the boiling point and odor descriptors of individual compounds comes from the good scents company database, http://www.thegoodscentscompany.com.

19 Jason Horn "Diacetyl: The Molecule Responsible for Butter Flavor ..." https://www.seriouseats.com/diacetyl-when-buttery-goodness-breaks-bad Accessed December 7, 2021

20 "The bacterium behind 'potato taste' in coffee..." Cirad. https://www.foreststreesagroforestry.org/news-article/cirad-the-bacterium-behind-potato-taste-in-coffee-has-been-identified/. Accessed December 7, 2021.

21 Bailey, Richard W (2004). "Part I - American English: its origins and history". In Edward Finegan; John R. Rickford (eds.). Language in the USA: Themes for the Twenty-first Century. Cambridge University Press

22 "Brewing Bavarian Weissbier ." Brau Magazin. https://braumagazin.de/article/brewing-bavarian-weissbier-all-you-ever-wanted-to-know/. Accessed June 18, 2020.

23 Asimov, Eric. "Brews as Complex as Wine" The New York Times. November 23, 2011, https://www.nytimes.com/2011/11/23/dining/sour-beers-review.html. Accessed June 19, 2020.

24 Nobutake Nunomura, Masaoki Sasaki, Yasuo Asao & Tamotsu Yokotsuka (1976) Isolation and Identification of 4-Hydroxy-2(or 5)-ethyl-5(or 2)-methyl-3(2H)-furanone, as a Flavor Component in Shoyu (Soy Sauce), Agricultural and Biological Chemistry, 40:3, 491-495, DOI: 10.1080/00021369.1976.10862083.

25 "Burnt Sugar Notes" Leffingwell & Associates. http://www.leffingwell.com/burnt.htm. Accessed June 21, 2020.

26 "Characterization of the Most Odor-Active Compounds..." June 21, 2008, https://pubs.acs.org/doi/10.1021/jf800382m. Accessed June 18, 2020.

27 "Aroma from Carotenoids - Rose." Leffingwell & Associates. http://www.leffingwell.com/rose.htm. Accessed June 18, 2020.

28 Toledo, P.R., Pezza, L., Pezza, H.R. and Toci, A.T. (2016), Relationship Between the Different Aspects Related to Coffee Quality and Their Volatile Compounds. COMPREHENSIVE REVIEWS IN FOOD SCIENCE AND FOOD SAFETY, 15: 705-719. https://doi.org/10.1111/1541-4337.12205. Accessed July 7, 2020.

29 "Quantitative Assessment of Citric Acid ..." National Center for Biotechnology Information. https://www.ncbi.nlm.nih.gov/pmc/articles/PMC2637791/. Accessed 32 August 7, 2020.

30 "Limonene: A target for Coffea arabica aromatic ... - Agritrop." http://agritrop.cirad.fr/593457/. Accessed August 7, 2020.

31 "I like buttery Chardonnay. Where does that flavor come from, and how do I find more of it?" Wine Spectator. October 10, 2012, https://wwwwinespectator.com/articles/i-like-buttery-chardonnay-where-does-that-flavor-come- from-and-how-do-i-find-more-of-it-47437. Accessed August 7, 2020.

32 Hendon, Christopher H., Colonna-Dashwood, Lesley, Colonna-Dashwood, Maxwell "The Role of Dissolved Cations in Coffee Extraction" https://pubs.acs.org/doi/pdf/10.1021/jf501687c. Accessed December 7, 2021

www.ingramcontent.com/pod-product-compliance
Ingram Content Group UK Ltd.
Pitfield, Milton Keynes, MK11 3LW, UK
UKHW021959270726
14060UKWH00003B/591

9 780578 341354